Ralph Barker started work as a journalist on the *Sporting Life* in 1935. He joined the RAF in 1940 and was subsequently granted a permanent commission, but he retired in 1961 to write full time. While still serving he wrote three books and became a regular contributor of feature articles to the *Sunday Express*, an association that has continued throughout his writing career. Most of his early books had an RAF background, but he has since written on a wide range of subjects, including mountaineering, terrorism and biography, as well as aviation and the sea. He lists cricket (about which he has written six books) and duplicate bridge as among his principal interests, and was a compulsive cricketer himself. This is his twenty-fourth book.

By the same author

RALPH BARKER

Children of the *Benares*

A War Crime and its Victims

'It is worse than a crime,
it is a blunder'
Boulay de la Meurthe

GRAFTON BOOKS
A Division of the Collins Publishing Group

LONDON GLASGOW
TORONTO SYDNEY AUCKLAND

Grafton Books
A Division of the Collins Publishing Group
8 Grafton Street, London W1X 3LA

Published by Grafton Books 1990

First published in Great Britain by
Methuen London Ltd 1987

A CIP catalogue record for this book is available
from the British Library

ISBN 0-586-20823-2

The map on p. 46, 'Route of Convoy OB 213,
13–17 September 1940', was drawn by Neil Hyslop

Printed and bound in Great Britain by
Collins, Glasgow

Set in Times

Contents

Illustrations

Acknowledgements

I am indebted first of all to the survivors, among both passengers and crew, who talked so generously and revealingly about their experiences before, during and after the sinking. Relatives of some of those who lost their lives in the sinking or have since died also gave invaluable help. Add to this the personal accounts and depositions written or recorded at the time, by passengers and crew members no longer alive, and I was able to reconstruct what happened aboard the vessel and afterwards in the lifeboats and on rafts in surprising detail after so long. Members of the crew of the destroyer HMS *Hurricane*, which picked up the bulk of the survivors, also gave vital information.

Through documents available at the Public Record Office at Kew, chiefly on Admiralty, Ministry of Transport and Dominions Office files, I was able to delineate the background against which the evacuation overseas of Britain's children took shape. The policy decisions which preceded and led to the sailing and sinking of the *City of Benares* are recorded in these files, as are the investigations, eventually aborted, that followed.

The log of *U48*, the U-boat which effected the sinking, was studied and the tactics of the U-boat commander probed, so far as that was possible. In this I was principally indebted to Captain Karl-Friedrich Merten, himself a U-boat commander in that period, and to the Naval Historical Branch of the Ministry of Defence.

Many other sources, personal and impersonal, have

helped in my reconstruction. The principal ones are listed in the Note on Sources on pp. 232–5. To them all, and to those not specifically mentioned or inadvertently omitted, I offer my grateful thanks. The interpretation in all cases is my own.

1

Welcome Aboard

Steaming westwards across the Atlantic at 8½ knots, bound for Halifax, Nova Scotia, the nineteen assorted vessels of slow convoy OB (ocean outbound) 213 were struggling to keep station, their problems exacerbated by their incompatible and polyglot composition and the rough seas and poor visibility they were encountering. Dutch, Greek, Algerian, British, Norwegian, tankers, freighters, whalers, tramps, banana boats – all were conforming as best they could to the speed predetermined by the convoy commodore, in essence the speed of the slowest. None wished, as they passed through the perilous North-Western Approaches, to be picked off as a straggler by some predatory U-boat. Arrayed on a broad front three miles across in eight columns of two vessels each, with an asymmetrical ninth column of three to vary the pattern, their generous spacing allowed them to zigzag safely in concert either side of their mean course to a prearranged schedule. This was their only defence, passive and ultimately predictable, against the submersible enemy, always suspected, always unseen.

It was not, however, their only protection. Three miles ahead, kept anxiously in focus by the crews of the merchantmen, the destroyer HMS *Winchelsea* zigzagged to an independent schedule, providing, through sophisticated listening devices, a continuous anti-submarine sweep. The pinging of her ASDIC (a submarine detection echo-sounding device), monitored by highly sensitive operators, was the convoy's essential warning of the presence of U-boats. With a sloop on either wing to complete the escort, the reward of any reckless U-boat commander venturing close enough to attack would be to be depth-charged.

Leading Column 5 – the centre column – was the commodore ship, the *City of Benares*, flagship of Ellerman's City Line. Completed in 1936, she was the largest and by far the most modern of that company's passenger liners, built on the Clyde for their Indian service. This was her first Atlantic crossing, and she had been fitted out specially for the purpose. Of distinctive, graceful appearance, with the hull lines of a yacht, she had a raked and rounded stern, two raked and tapering masts, and two elliptical funnels; but her beauty was somewhat marred by her wartime camouflage of buff superstructure and blackened hull. Her gross tonnage was 11,081 and her maximum speed 15 knots. Propelled by two coal-burning Parsons turbines developing 1,450 horse-power, driving through single reduction mechanical gearing, she was 509 feet in overall length, 62 feet 7 inches in beam, and had a moulded depth of 43¼ feet. Built to Lloyd's first-class-plus specifications, she stood out in present company; but this, in the circumstances in which she found herself, might not be an advantage. Her employment for the task to which she was committed had followed much heart-searching.

So too had her sailing date – Friday, 13 September 1940. Few seamen, even in peacetime, cared to sail on such a reputedly unlucky day, and in wartime it almost seemed like tempting fate. Her departure in ob 213 (thirteen again) had been scheduled for Thursday the 12th, but mines sown in the Mersey by the *Luftwaffe* had delayed her sailing. Any further postponement, however, would have held up her naval escort, making it late for its rendezvous in four days' time with an incoming convoy from Canada, which it was part of its operational duty to meet. So Friday the 13th it had to be.

Far and away the most protracted agonizing, however, lasting many months, concerned her cargo, precious to the point of the incalculable and conferring on captain and crew, and on all those connected with the voyage, an awesome responsibility. For her present role the *City of Benares* was partly in ballast, her passenger capacity reduced from her peacetime maximum to around 200 – 100 adults and 100 children. Last-minute cancellations had reduced the adults to ninety-one, but the full complement of 100 children had been embarked.

Ten of these children, the offspring of parents who could afford to pay, had had their passages booked privately. The other ninety, less favoured perhaps by fortune, were sailing under a government-sponsored scheme for the evacuation to private homes in the Dominions of children between the ages of five and sixteen attending, in most cases, grant-aided schools. They were part of the vanguard of the many thousands of such children, selected from the most vulnerable areas of Great Britain, whom it was hoped to despatch, under special arrangements prepared by the Children's Overseas Reception Board (CORB), to safe havens in Canada, Australia, New Zealand and South Africa, and also under a separate scheme to the United States, all of whom were generously offering to help.

The exodus of the *Benares* party coincided with the climax of the Battle of Britain. After attempting to eliminate airfields and ports, Goering had switched the *Luftwaffe* to an all-out attack on London, and on the day/night of 7/8 September more than 400 Londoners were killed and over 1,000 injured. The blitz on the capital city continued at this level, and the threatened Nazi invasion looked imminent. Against these evils, half-demented parents had to weigh the hazards of ocean travel in wartime. All restrictions on submarine warfare, although imposed by solemn treaty, had been abandoned by the enemy.

The sponsoring authority, in their communications to parents, had not minimized the dangers, but to the children, thrilled at the prospect of seeing and growing up in the New World, the perils of the passage were part of the adventure. Would they rather be bombed or torpedoed? On the whole they thought they would prefer the latter – they would be sure to be rescued. Parents were swayed by their pleading, and by the feeling that to resist would be to deny them the chance of a lifetime, perhaps even the chance of life itself. But the decisive factor, for those who applied on behalf of their children, was an assurance by the government that all ships carrying evacuated children under the scheme would be convoyed, and that if for any reason this proved impracticable, the arrangements for sailing would be cancelled and parents notified.

Implicit in these assurances was that the children would enjoy the protection of the Royal Navy. This, Britain's senior service, was more than a mere fleet of ships. It was a *corps d'élite*, a focus of patriotism, an island tradition, in which parents and children shared a sublime, unshakeable faith. The assurances given, for most of the waverers, resolved the dilemma.

The adult passengers on the *Benares* were a colourful mixture of the cosmopolitan, the intellectual and the persecuted. Some were travelling on business, seen as essential for the earning of dollars, some were joining relatives in Canada or the States, some were genuine refugees. Arthur Wimperis, a distinguished West End playwright and scriptwriter, was joining Alexander Korda in Hollywood to work on a film scenario; he had worked with Korda before, notably on *The Private Life of Henry VIII*. Alderman William Golightly, president of the Northumberland Miners' Association, was attending a Labour Trade Convention in Canada. Lieutenant-Colonel James Baldwin-Webb, MP for the Wrekin, was on a mission to New York to raise money for ambulances for the British Red Cross; large, genial and resonant of voice, he was almost a caricature of the ex-soldier MP. But he would be at his best in a crisis.

Marion Day was going to Canada to get married. Engaged to a Canadian pilot who had been killed in the RAF, she had met his brother at the funeral and soon afterwards agreed to marry him instead.

Florence Croasdaile, an American girl, now thirty-eight, had married an officer in the British merchant navy at St Martin-in-the-Fields twelve years earlier. When her husband was torpedoed off the Norwegian coast and taken prisoner she responded to her mother's invitation to take the two children – Patricia, nine, and Lawrence, two – to America for the duration. It seemed the sensible thing to do.

Alice Grierson, thirty-six, a slight but attractive figure, always in slacks and with a cigarette dangling from her lips, was filming the day-to-day activities of the evacuee children for the Canadian government. Like some latter-day pied piper she was tracked relentlessly by children wanting to get into the film. Another communicator, thirty-two-year-old Eric Davis, of the BBC, was on his way to an appointment in Malaya. Definitely a non-communicator was French Air Force Lieutenant Hervé de Kerillis, on a secret mission to Quebec.

Among the refugees were some twenty aliens, forced to flee from Nazi persecution in Europe. Hungarians, Poles, Germans, Czechs, they were a distinguished group, many of them writers, historians and journalists. The stateless Rudolf Olden, pacifist and Jew, had been hounded out of Germany in 1934 for opposing Hitler in his newspaper *Berliner Tageblatt*, only to be interned in Britain with his wife Ika, like many others of his kind, on the outbreak of war. Subsequently released, he and Ika would be joining their two-year-old daughter Mary, who had travelled ahead of them and was being cared for by friends in Toronto.

Monika Lanyi, travelling with her husband, an art historian, was a daughter of the German author Thomas Mann.

Only a handful of the children, those who had actually been bombed out of their homes, could correctly be called refugees. Among those unfortunates, however, were five children of one family, the Grimmonds, whose council house in Brixton had been reduced to rubble by a direct hit on the third night of the London blitz, Monday, 9 September. Mercifully the whole family, which consisted of Eddie Grimmond, his wife Hannah, and their ten children, had retired for the night to their Anderson shelter (named after the contemporary Home Secretary), which they had specially enlarged by do-it-yourself digging to accommodate the children in bunks. Although in those first three nights more than 1,000 Londoners were killed, the Grimmonds escaped unharmed. But they lost all their possessions, including the tightly crammed suitcases, holding a poignant mixture of the old, the handed-down and the new, which the five children entered under the government scheme were due to take with them to the reception centre next morning. All five were on the reserve list to travel on the *City of Benares*.

'They can't possibly go without their clothes,' was the reaction of Hannah Grimmond. But welfare staff promised to re-fit them, and the argument that their homelessness made their evacuation all the more urgent was a difficult one to resist. Eddie Grimmond, a crusher labourer employed by Southwark Council, had been a machine-gunner in the First World War (he had joined up at sixteen), and the bombing had awakened vivid memories of the trenches. He had seen his best friend killed beside him in France and had come home, in the course of time, to marry his widow, taking on one step-child and adding nine of his own. On that dust-laden, rubble-strewn morning he told his wife that from what he knew of the Jerries the bombing would only get worse. Here at least, he argued, was a chance to save five of the Grimmond family. Reluctantly, Hannah Grimmond agreed that they should go.

The lucky children, as it seemed, were the five whose ages were over five and under sixteen. Augusta (Gussie), the eldest of them and a self-appointed 'little mother' to the others, was thirteen. Violet was ten, Connie nine, Eddie junior eight, Lenny five. Pinched and pallid with shock, they were delivered by their father to the rail terminus by taxi, and later that day they travelled north to Liverpool, their specially recruited escorts cleaning them up and re-equipping them as best they could on the way.

At their destination they were bedded down with scores of other government-sponsored evacuee children – sea-vacuees, they were called – in emergency dormitories – classrooms converted into bedrooms – at the Sherwood's Lane Senior Girls' School in the Fazackerley District of

Liverpool, well away from the docks and therefore considered reasonably safe. But that night, in common with most nights of the period, the air-raid sirens sounded and the children, numbering over 100 including reserves, were roused and urged to run for the shelters. These were above surface in the school grounds, with spare bedding, so once the children left the school they were told to stay in the shelters and complete their night's rest without further disturbance.

Reinforcing this policy was an anti-aircraft battery sited near the school, which peppered the grounds with shrapnel during a raid. Returning next morning for breakfast in the school hall, the children delighted in collecting chunks of shrapnel as souvenirs. The largest and most jagged lump was seized by a boy named Derek Capel, from Hanworth in Middlesex; he displayed it proudly to his younger brother Alan, who was five. Derek regarded the shrapnel as a talisman, and he was not in the least abashed at the eventual date of the sailing; 13 was his lucky number.

Characters among the children were already emerging as they savoured their temporary billet – as noted with admiration and amusement by Margaret Abraham, headmistress of the school. The kindly Cockney tyranny exercised by Gussie Grimmond over her charges stood out; they had to do as they were told. They still had no clothes other than those rustled together by their escorts and, stimulated by Margaret Abraham, the Sherwood's Lane schoolgirls brought a selection of clothing for them. When she learnt that these five bombed-out children were languishing on the reserve list, she successfully urged the sponsoring authority to promote them to the accepted list. It was an action she was to remember all her life.

Another girl who attracted Margaret Abraham's attention was Rosemary Spencer-Davies, aged fifteen. She too came from Brixton. She really comforted the younger children and prevailed upon her brother John, who was nine, to help her. All that summer their mother had resisted the idea of sea evacuation but her husband, a Post Office engineer, wanted to get both children away before Rosemary's sixteenth birthday made her ineligible for the scheme. As the threat of invasion mounted, his wife finally agreed. But the letter calling the children forward was delayed, ironically enough, in the post, leaving less than two hours to get the children packed and transported to the train. Only after a frantic effort did they make it. Even in that euphoric moment, Mrs Spencer-Davies almost regretted it.

Rosemary was not only one of the oldest of the children, she was also one of the most mature. Shapely and slender, talented and artistic, she had been highly commended for her entry in a painting competition run by a newspaper and had also been awarded an RSPCA certificate of merit for an essay on kindness to animals. John, too, had an artistic bent, enlivened by a keen sense of the ridiculous. In a sketched depiction of a Battle of Britain dogfight, he drew an instantly recognizable visage on a bloated barrage balloon of Hermann Goering.

Rosemary and John were on the accepted list, which was inevitably dominated by children from the London area. Two more fugitives from Brixton, where they lived in a council flat, were Jack and Joyce Keeley, eight and six respectively. Jack was a boy with an active mind who never stopped talking, while Joyce was homesick from the first and kept asking to go back. Robert and John Baker, twelve and seven, from Southall, were going to stay with an aunt on a farm in Saskatchewan, and they were day-dreaming of an open-air life on the prairie and exciting trips to the Rockies.

There were parties of a dozen or so from three provincial areas which had come under *Luftwaffe* fire: Cardiff and Newport, Sunderland, and Liverpool itself. The two oldest of the Sunderland children were the bouncing, self-assured Eleanor Wright, whose fascination with Canada had been inspired by a pen-friend in Prince Edward Island; and George Crawford, a boy scout of tenacious temperament and robust physique. Both went to the Bede School, both were thirteen. Another Sunderland girl, nine-year-old Dorothy Wood, was given the chance to withdraw when her young brother, who had travelled with her to Liverpool, fell ill, but she pleaded with her parents and they let her go.

Two girls from different areas and of contrasting temperament who nevertheless found much in common, both physically – they were plump – and in interests and inclination, were Beth Cummings of Liverpool and Bess Walder of Kentish Town, London. Extrovert and warm-hearted, Beth had been brought up by a loving mother after her father was killed in an accident when she was three. Bess was more restrained but of similar enthusiasms, and they vowed to stick together come what may. Beth was fourteen and Bess, who wore glasses (she could see nothing without them), fifteen. Bess had her younger brother Louis travelling with her – he was ten – but an early segregation of the sexes made contact intermittent.

Escorts for the sponsored children, carefully selected from many thousands of volunteers, were provided at the rate of one to each group of fifteen, plus one reserve, together with a senior escort, a doctor and a qualified nurse. To complement these the *Benares* carried a ship's surgeon and five stewardess/nurses (unqualified) specially recruited by Purser John Anderson, a phlegmatic Aberdonian. The senior escort, Marjorie Day, was a housemistress at a girls' school in Buckinghamshire, and all the escorts were either women teachers or clergymen, except for twenty-three-year-old Michael Rennie, who was using the vacation between his degree course at Keble College, Oxford and his training for ordination to make a noncombatant contribution to the war effort. Rennie, a descendant of John Rennie, the Scottish civil engineer and bridge designer, displayed all the cheerful ebullience of the embryo curate, and his wide experience of coping with boys in the sea scouts was expected to be useful. The doctor, thirty-year-old Margaret Zeal, had been granted special leave from Hammersmith Hospital; her first surgical task was to repair the cracked skull of a doll belonging to eight-year-old Patricia Harrington from Wembley, an operation she performed with due professional care.

The staff of Sherwood's Lane School did all in their power to care for the children who had been billeted on them almost without warning, accepting the disruption of the curriculum, the displacement of pupils and the inevitable chaos inside the school, all greatly exacerbated by the sailing delay. Some of the children, fractious and homesick, found the surroundings depressing and the food unappetizing or insufficient. Seven-year-old John Snoad was one of many children comforted by Rosemary Spencer-Davies, but he found the two nights he spent in the shelters at the Fazackerley school the grimmest of his life. There weren't enough camp beds to go round, and he slept on a palliasse on the bare floor, huddled together with other children of his age, listening to the bombs falling and the rats scratching. The result was a heavy asthmatic cold, which caused him to fail the stringent medical examination performed by British and Canadian doctors in tandem prior to boarding. Two days later, minus most of his luggage, he was pushed out of a taxi outside his home in Tooting, to the astonishment of his mother who imagined him already halfway across the Atlantic.

These children would have envied the privately booked children, most of whom were staying at the Adelphi, Liverpool's most famous hotel. But even they finished up cowering in the wine cellars at night. Among them were the Bech children – Barbara, fourteen, Sonia, eleven, and Derek, nine – who were accompanied by their mother. Marguerite Bech had horrendous childhood memories of the Zeppelin raids of the First World War. Married to a Dane – he was managing director of the Royal Danish Porcelain Company in New Bond Street – she had been determined to get the children away from the battle area on the Sussex coast, where the hardware collected by Derek was ample evidence of the proximity of the air fighting. Hating to be parted from his treasures, the boisterous Derek had brought a macabre selection along with him. Sonia for her part displayed with equal pride her new camel-hair coat, bought at a London store just before sailing. Barbara, the eldest, was leaving under protest: she resented being uprooted from her teenage friends and felt guilty at running away.

Her attitude was by no means unique. One Eton schoolboy, teased by his classmates, played truant from the Cunard liner on which he had been privately booked and like some disillusioned escaped prisoner found his way back to school.

*   *   *

While in port at Liverpool the *City of Benares* underwent a full survey for the renewal of her passenger certificate, during which machinery, boilers and emergency generator were tested and all life-saving appliances checked. The boat falls were found in good condition, double painters were fitted to each boat, and none of them leaked. Each of her twelve boats was lowered to the water and water-tested, buoyancy tanks were examined and found to be well built and well maintained, and each boat was fitted with Fleming hand-propelling gear and Schat skids. The Fleming gear consisted of ten hand-levers mounted inside the boat, five on the port side and five on the starboard, which drove a shaft running along the keel to a propeller astern; as a means of propulsion it was superior in passenger vessels to oars, which only a strong and experienced sailor could handle. All boats had two or three oars shipped as well. The Schat skids were fitted to minimize damage to the side planking of the boats through hammering against the ship's shell-plates in the case of an adverse list.

The total capacity of the boats was 494 persons, a margin of eighty-eight over the aggregate of passengers and crew (406), and there were twenty-two rafts and eighteen lifebuoys. In addition to the standard cork life-jackets, available for everyone, Ellerman's had supplied small kapok vests for each child. 'I can safely say,' concluded the Ministry of Shipping surveyor, 'that the boats and their equipment were all that could be desired . . . I would add that the owners' representatives showed themselves most desirous to do everything in the interests of safety.'

The only note of dubiety expressed by the port authority concerned the high ratio of Asian to European male crew: the latter were outnumbered by more than four to one. Already there had been misgivings about the suitability of Lascars (as Asian crews were known) for Atlantic crossings, to which they had been unaccustomed until recently. 'I discussed the question with the owners' representatives with a view to getting more Europeans,' wrote a Ministry of Shipping inspector, 'but it seems this presents considerable difficulty.' It was during these discussions that Ellerman's agreed to limit the number of sponsored children to ninety and of fare-paying children to ten. 'This,' said the inspector, 'certainly ameliorated the position.'

The term Lascar covered all seamen of Asian – usually East Indian – origin employed on European ships. The word probably originated from the Hindi *lashkar* (army), and was also reminiscent of *askari*, the European-trained African soldier. Lascars were docile, disciplined and hardworking, and were highly regarded by marine superintendents. On routes in the Northern Hemisphere their efficiency was rated lower than that of Europeans, but with proper supervision their performance was regarded as acceptable. They had proved their steadfastness under pressure in the First World War.

At last, on the morning of Thursday, 12 September, the Sherwood's Lane School was vacated and the evacuee children were taken by bus to the docks, leaving Margaret Abraham and her staff to clear the school and their minds of accumulated debris and get back to an interval of normal schooling before the arrival of the next batch of evacuees. At Prince's Landing Stage the children had barely swallowed the mandatory milk and biscuits and had their bags examined by Customs when there was yet another air raid and they were herded into a nearby shelter. It was a timely reminder of the dangers they were leaving behind. Community singing was obligatory during these troglodyte excursions, but after twenty minutes the all-clear sounded and the children embarked, with the odd flutter of misgiving, on the *City of Benares*. There was no recanting now. Their simple courage earned them enthusiastic acclamation from the crew of the ship that lay in the adjacent berth, the *Duchess of Atholl*; she was crammed with British sailors on their way to Halifax to crew fifty obsolete but reconditioned American destroyers for which Churchill had traded a clutch of bases in the Caribbean. The agreement had been signed on 7 September. Britain desperately needed the destroyers; and if the exchange was hardly an equal one, it meant, to Churchill, another step towards the much-desired involvement of America in the war.

Welcomed on board by the ship's company, the children were shown round the *Benares* before being led to their accommodation. This was aft on the main deck, the lowest occupied deck, above which were three more decks: in ascending order they were the upper deck (so called); the promenade deck, where all the public rooms except the dining-room were situated (they also served as muster stations); and the boat or bridge deck. The boys, forty-six of them, were on the starboard side, the girls, forty-four of them, on the port side. Each set of cabins opened on to a corridor, with bathrooms between the two corridors. The Asian crew were also accommodated aft, in the poop, which gave the children a powerful smell of curry to inhale around mealtimes.

The *Benares* was a single-class ship, but the accommodation of the paying passengers forward ensured virtual segregation. This had been requested not by Ellerman's but by CORB; restricting evacuee children and their escorts to one section of the ship made supervision easier.

All forty-three cabins in the aft part of the ship, totalling over a hundred berths, were reserved for them, and the escorts and the stewardess/nurses recruited by John Anderson were also accommodated there. The dining-room, on the upper deck amidships, was used for meals but at staggered times, and the children had exclusive use of the children's playroom, the verandah café on the sports deck, and the area immediately behind it. As the swimming pool was boarded in, adequate space was provided for games and exercise. The arrangements also suited the cabin-class passengers, protecting them from the possible annoyance of ninety milling evacuee children – slum children, in the eyes of some – having the run of the ship.

The master, Captain Landles Nicoll, of Arbroath (Landles, or Landless, because he had been born at sea), Chief Engineer Alex Macauley, and First Radio Officer Alistair Fairweather, met the commodore at the convoy conference at the local Admiralty offices in the Royal Liver Building at two-thirty that afternoon. When they returned two hours later the *Benares* had left the landing stage and anchored in mid-river to wait for the channel to be cleared, and they joined her via the Admiral's barge. The crew consisted of 166 Lascars and 43 British – mostly Scots – of whom five (the chief stewardess and four nurse/stewardesses) were women. Among the British crew were four DEMS (Defensively Equipped Merchant Ships) gunners to man the six-inch and three-inch guns mounted in the stern. The total number of fare-paying passengers was ninety-one including children; there were 100 from CORB including escorts; and the balance of six was made up by the convoy staff.

The convoy commodore, Admiral Edmund Mackinnon, DSO, RN (retired), aged 60, had been recalled for war service; after serving with distinction in the First World War he had retired in 1933. His staff comprised four naval hand-signallers and a telegraphist, who soon found that under longish grey hair and an erect, formidable bearing was what they called 'a thorough gentleman', a man of few words who nevertheless went out of his way to get to know them and their problems and always addressed them by name. They saw him, too, as very much a man with a mind of his own.

Mackinnon's responsibilities were for the convoy as a whole, but this included the *Benares*, a situation which inevitably left room for differences of opinion with Captain Nicoll. With one man controlling the destiny of 19 merchant ships up to the point of dispersal, and the other principally concerned with the safety of the 191 passengers in his care, of whom 100 were children, these differences could well acuminate into a clash. The *Benares* was a ship with two captains.

Meanwhile the escorts were briefed in their duties, and copies of typewritten instructions on emergency drills and 'Abandon Ship' procedures were distributed to them. They were enjoined, in an emergency, 'to see that the children get their lifebelts and suitable clothing and proceed to the assembly station allotted to each group'. Four separate emergency and fire drills were held for everyone on board, with a Ministry of Shipping surveyor present. At these drills passengers wore their life-jackets and the children their life-jackets over the kapok waistcoats. Each life-jacket was inspected and declared serviceable. The children were mustered and their assembly stations and lifeboats allotted to them. At the last of these drills, two of the boats were lowered to the promenade deck and some of the children were put into them, watched by the others. Reprovisioning of boats and rafts was checked, watertight doors were tested. The *Benares*, it seemed, was prepared for the worst.

It was immediately noticed, on the morning of the 13th, that the *Duchess of Atholl* had sailed, so the inference was that the channel must have been cleared. But for some hours afterwards the port remained closed. The day spent in mid-river, in contact with land, gave the children a welcome extension for writing home. None were more prolific than the Grimmonds, led and coerced by Gussie. Scrawny and angular, but chirpy and quick-witted, she could see the funny side of things. Her letter paints an endearing picture of the Grimmond family as a unit. This is what she wrote:

Dear Mum and Dad,

It is very lovely here on the ship. I wish you were with us. We have men from Calcutta to wait on us, and we go into a big room for meals and we have silver knives and forks – table napkins and *three different kinds* of knives and forks. We have a menu card in which we can choose what we like off the card. There are about a dozen different things on it.

We had our photo taken as we were coming on the boat, and we are going to have it taken again now. We are drinking milk in the Lounge. Our boat is in the middle of the river. We are all eager to start off.

While we were on the boat last night there were two air raid warnings, but we were asleep.

We have plenty of dark men on this boat. They clean our shoes and clean our room for us. They do all the work when we are on deck. The dark men look at us, but we don't take any notice. You have to laugh at the way they are dressed. Some have their shirts hanging out. They have no shoes.

Here the alarm bells called the children to yet another lifeboat drill, and she had to break off. It was rumoured that the ship would be sailing at one-thirty that afternoon. The children's lunch, which Gussie quite rightly called dinner – it was the children's main meal – was served at eleven-thirty, after which she continued her letter:

Dear Dad,

I started this letter before dinner and am just finishing it. I have just found out that we might not be sailing at one-thirty, we might be sailing at one o'clock tonight. [She had evidently been pumping a somewhat noncommittal member of the crew.] It's all according to the tide.

Eddie and Lenny are sharing a cabin. Connie, Violet and me are sharing a cabin. The cabins are all furnished. Connie and Violet are sharing a wardrobe.

We have had three practices of life drill in case our boat got hit. The little ones have got a nursery to play in and a big store sent them a box of toys. Lenny goes about as if nothing had happened.

Please, Mum, do not worry as we have been fitted up with clothes. Our escort is a very nice lady, Miss Cornish, but we call her Auntie Mary. [Mary Cornish, a forty-one-year-old music teacher, had quickly gained the confidence and affection of her girls.]

There are men to guard us at night in case our boat got sunk. Please do not answer this letter as I will be in mid-Atlantic. Excuse writing and spelling.

Goodbye must close now from your loving Gussie and from the others, give our love to the others.

Your loving daughter Gussie
XXXX

Gussie saw to it that Violet and Connie wrote too. 'I hope you are all right, we are all right too,' wrote Violet. 'We have good food. We have a play room to play in. We have life practices in case our ship got sunk. We would put lifebelts on and jump into our lifeboats.'

Connie wrote: 'I hope you are all right. Me, Gussie and Violet feed the seagulls with biscuits [spelt bissets]. When Lenny went on deck we saw seagulls swimming in the water and fighting. When we was having milk the bells went for every baby to go and put on lifebelts. I bet Jimmy and Jerry [the two youngest Grimmond children] miss us. Goodbye from your loving daughter Connie.' The remainder of the page was filled with kisses.

At six o'clock that evening, Friday, 13 September, the *City of Benares* put to sea. All watertight doors were closed, all lifeboats were swung to the outboard position on the boat deck for rapid lowering in emergency, and all rafts were placed in position. The atmosphere among the children was one of carefree excitement, infecting if not wholly suborning the adults. All the way down the Mersey, until their escorts drove them to bed, they shouted and waved at ships at anchor and were cheered and saluted in return. There was certainly no secrecy about their departure.

As they moved out of the Mersey into the bay, the wind blew more strongly, the sea roughened, and the mood in the aft cabins changed. That night the *Benares* began to roll, and to Beth Cummings, sharing a cabin with two other Liverpool girls – her new friend Bess Walder was in the next cabin – the ship seemed almost to be looping the loop. First her companions – Joan Irving (fifteen) and Betty Unwin (twelve) – and then Beth herself, felt queer. The stewardess appeared and gave each girl a tin of barley sugar, but on Saturday morning they all felt decidedly queasy. Nearly all the evacuee children were the same, adding seasickness to the home-sickness that was succeeding excitement for some. Escort for the Liverpool girls was forty-four-year-old Maud Hill-man, an infant teacher, and 'quite a genius with the children', in the eyes of senior escort Marjorie Day. She was doubly enthusiastic about the voyage as she would be joining her husband in Canada. 'Try to eat something, you'll feel better for it,' she told them, and Beth, after getting some fresh air on deck, went down to the dining-room. But she ate little, and soon the saloon began to revolve. With others she made a rush for the sports deck, where she found a quiet spot with Bess Walder. When a scare that a German bomber was tracking them brought orders from the escorts to go below to their cabins they pretended to be asleep and got away with it. It was a ruse they were to employ whenever it suited them, mostly with success.

They found Maud Hillman a sympathetic escort, ready to give the older girls all the freedom she could. She was firmer with the younger ones, the smallest of whom were a brother and sister, Joan and James Spencer, aged seven and five respectively. In any group of children their flaxen hair stood out.

Joined by vessels from Bristol and the Clyde, Convoy OB 213 formed up off Rathlin Island into its nine appointed columns, with the commodore ship centre-front. She was the biggest and most attractive ship in the convoy, and the only one with the facilities to act as commodore ship. The escort of a destroyer and two sloops, with a Sunderland flying-boat in attendance at the outset, was modest enough, but it was standard for the period. Whether it met the government's precept that naval protection should reasonably ensure the safety of the evacuee children remained to be shown.

Captain Nicoll, for one, was doubtful. Strong and squarely built, even stocky, with wiry hair greying at the temples but not receding, he was very much the pro-fessional seaman and navigator, content with his lot, self-sufficient, something of a man apart, but sociable enough in the company of friends. He was fifty-one. A good family man, he had admitted to misgivings, amounting almost to a premonition, about this Atlantic crossing to the eldest of his three daughters before leaving Arbroath. 'If only we could get away by ourselves at sea,' he told her, 'just the *Benares* on her own, I could employ a zigzag course at high speed and we would have a better chance.' He was thinking not of himself but of his passengers and crew and of his ship. 'I've had a good life,' he told his daughter, 'whatever's in store for me I can't complain.' He said nothing of this to his wife, but she knew without being told that if the worst happened he would go down with his ship.

Asked by a stylish couple sitting at the captain's table – the Digby-Mortons, Henry (thirty-eight) and Phyllis (thirty-four), on their way to the States for a six-week fashion tour sponsored by the Board of Trade – why his own two younger daughters weren't on board, he intoned his reply so that only they could hear. 'I'd as soon put their hands in the fire.'

Phyllis Digby-Morton thought the whole scheme for sponsoring evacuee children was an aberration, thrust on the government by an excess of egalitarianism. Parents who wanted to send their children abroad and could afford the fare should possibly be allowed to do so, if shipping space was available and if they thought it worth the risk. But she had no patience with encouraging parents in what she regarded as folly.

Although rough weather marred the children's enjoyment at first, recovery was swift. Two suspected cases of chickenpox – one was the five-year-old Alan Capel, from Hanworth, younger brother of Derek, the boy with the outsize piece of shrapnel whose lucky number was 13 – were quarantined in the hospital on the boat deck, but by Sunday the 15th nearly everyone had found their sea legs and they had the time and the stomach to savour the contrast between the sombre drabness of the war-torn, blacked-out back streets they mostly came from and the fairyland glitter and gloss of a luxury passenger liner. No longer did they regard the 'dark men' with suspicion. The kindness and attention they were shown were totally disarming. To have their chairs pushed in for them by these strikingly handsome waiters – they soon learned to call them stewards – with their pale blue and white uniforms and ornate blue sashes, was a continual delight. And after wartime rationing – eight ounces of sugar per week, eight ounces of fats, two ounces of cheese, eight ounces of bacon and a minuscule portion of meat – the children turned every meal into a banquet, while the stewards were their willing accomplices in serving both alternative courses where the menu provided a choice. Most popular of all were the gargantuan helpings of ice cream which brought the two main meals of the day to repletion.

Mealtimes kept Gussie Grimmond particularly busy. First she had to decide for herself which item it was best to select from the profusion of courses and cutlery, then, eager to do the right thing and ashamed of any solecisms of deportment or table manners committed by her charges that might 'show them up', she corrected or cajoled them as she thought proper, all this to a background of unself-conscious chatter and laughter. The Grimmonds, at least, were never allowed to be greedy.

Once the children got over their nausea, lifeboat drills were held daily, and on Sunday Rev. William H. King, twenty-eight, from Hamilton, Ontario, returning to Canada as a CORB escort, took morning service on the sports deck, at which the children sang 'Eternal Father, Strong to Save'. This had an unforeseen effect on the impressionable Beth Cummings, who shuddered at the perils the hymn conjured up in her mind. Sunday lunch

cheered everyone up, and the older children did their best
to play truant when the escorts ordered them to their
cabins for an afternoon rest.

Attention to spiritual needs was supposed to be shared
between King, a Protestant, and a Roman Catholic priest
named Roderick (Rory) O'Sullivan, to avoid any charge
of sectarian bias. O'Sullivan, who was thirty-two, was a
member of the Order of St Francis de Sales and had been
teaching at St Michael's College, Annecy, on the French/
Swiss border, when France capitulated. He escaped to
England in a small boat from Bordeaux and applied at
once for a naval chaplaincy, but had to be satisfied with
being put on the waiting list. He had volunteered to act
as an escort meanwhile. However, he was so affected by
seasickness that Padre King took all the services.

Most active in organizing deck games was the theological student Michael Rennie; he kept his boys amused by
supervising tugs-of-war and teaching them the art of
lassoing. Mary Cornish had Rosemary Spencer-Davies in
her party, and she continued to help with the younger
ones; the quiet but strong personality of 'Auntie Mary'
Cornish inspired all the girls to help each other. Also in
her party were Eleanor Wright and three other Sunderland girls, two of whom, sisters Edith and Irene Smith,
made it their task to care for the third and youngest, six-
year-old Ann Watson. This attractive child's hair was a
mass of blonde curls, each one tied up in a ribbon, giving
the Smith girls endless absorption; they played with her
like a doll.

On that Sunday there were two radioed warnings of U-
boats in the vicinity of the convoy, and consultation
between Admiral Mackinnon and the senior officer of the
escort on HMS *Winchelsea* brought frequent changes of
course. There was a scare, too, that one of the dreaded

Focke-Wulf Condors, the long-range converted airliners
that spotted for U-boat targets and often bombed ships
on their own account – 'the scourge of the Atlantic',
Churchill called them – was on patrol nearby, but nothing
was sighted. Nevertheless the gunners, among whom
Harry Peard, a thirty-eight-year-old Bristolian, was the
smallest at 5 feet 4 inches, as well as the oldest and most
loquacious, and the look-outs on the bridge, in the crow's
nest, and on the forecastle head, redoubled their
vigilance.

By Monday most of the children had settled happily
into the shipboard routine. After breakfast they assembled for prayers with Padre King on the sports deck, and
then senior escort Marjorie Day read out the news and
the notices, with details of any special entertainments.
Letter-writing was a popular activity, there were routine
interruptions for lifeboat drill, and at tea-time Alice
Grierson shot some more film. There were still a few
children laid low by seasickness, among them Beth Cummings's cabin companion Joan Irving, who stayed in bed
all day, but most had their sea legs by now.

Although constantly under surveillance, the children
managed to gape now and then at the fare-paying passengers, mostly foreign intellectuals and well-to-do British,
who looked to them like creatures from another world, as
indeed they were. The zoo-like interest, however, was not
all one way, Arthur Wimperis being one of several who
watched the evacuee children at play. He was not one of
those who dismissed them as slum kids, indeed he thought
them clear-eyed, good-looking, fine specimens of English
– and Welsh – childhood, the best possible ambassadors
for the Old Country.

For the adults, as for the children, there was a general
easing of tension, though few remarked on it, fearing to

speak too soon; passengers went on assuring each other that 'we're not out of the wood yet'. Most U-boat attacks on Atlantic shipping occurred off the north-west Irish coast or within 300 miles of it, and although there had recently been incidents farther west, the area known to be infested with U-boats was disappearing astern.

There was also heart-warming news from home, thrilling beyond measure: the RAF were claiming to have shot down a record 185 German planes the previous day, a triumph that was enthusiastically applauded when it was announced on the ship. Even the refugees had deep anxieties about friends and relatives left behind in Europe, and they joined in the general rejoicing.

The atmosphere was not quite carefree, but the planning of competitive games, and a tea party organized that afternoon for the sponsored children, were symptomatic, contributing to a more relaxed mood. Escorts and stewardesses, backed up by cooks and stewards, made food and entertainment memorable, the dining-room was festooned, and there were crackers and paper hats for each child. That night they were allowed to undress on going to bed, provided they retained their kapok waistcoats and their clothing ready to hand.

For the first time the children slept soundly, but the party atmosphere did not survive the night. They were dismayed to find, when they awoke on the morning of Tuesday, 17 September, that the wind had risen and the heavens were darkened by angry clouds which brought sleeting rain. The more the ship rolled the less they felt like eating – breakfast, dinner or tea. Yet it was the adults who suffered the greater shock. They discovered that during the hours of darkness the naval escort had gone.

In vain did they scan the horizon. Nineteen ships were grimly counted, still struggling to keep station, some unsuccessfully, but *Winchelsea* and the two sloops had abandoned them. Or was it only a temporary decampment, to fend off some incipient attack? They learned at breakfast that it was not.

The defection was no surprise to Admiral Mackinnon, or to Captain Nicoll. They had known before sailing what the limit of escort would be – about 17 degrees West – and they knew too that it was immutable, because of a requirement to meet and escort through the treacherous North-Western Approaches an incoming convoy from Halifax, laden with armaments, equipment and stores. This was Convoy HX 71. In fact the escort had stayed with OB 213 rather longer than Mackinnon had had any right to expect. Scheduled to depart at 22.00 on the night of the 16th, the escort commander had been able to extend this to 01.00 on the 17th because HX 71 was marginally late. Mackinnon and Nicoll had watched them go.

Had this 'limit of convoy', as it was known, governed as it was by the number and endurance of available warships, been known to parents beforehand, it seems doubtful whether they would have suffered their children to sail.

During the seven years since Mackinnon's retirement from active service, convoy work and the threats to it, on the surface and beneath it, had changed little; indeed the bulk of experience had been gained during the First World War. Mackinnon was abreast of what changes there were, and so far as the air threat was concerned they would shortly be beyond Condor range. But he knew well enough that a convoy without the escort of warships, and therefore without ASDIC, was easy meat for any patrolling U-boat that might pick them up. Indeed, strictly speaking it wasn't a convoy at all.

Mackinnon's orders were to disperse his convoy at

midday on the 17th, after which ships' were to continue independently to their various destinations. No ship's crew was more impatient for dispersal than that of the *City of Benares*; their maximum speed was not far short of double the 8½ knots of the convoy. Nicoll himself, as already noted, would have plumped for a lone crossing at his best speed if he'd had his way – as would CORB and Ellerman's – but they had been overruled.

Precisely what passed between Mackinnon and Nicoll at this point is uncertain, but that the clash that had always seemed possible did actually occur is confirmed by Signalman Johnny Mayhew, today the sole survivor of the Admiral's staff. Asked by his immediate superior, the chief yeoman of signals, a man named Bartlett, to fetch his greatcoat from the chart room some time after midday ('It's getting a bit chilly,' said Bartlett.), Mayhew heard voices as he reached and opened the chart-room door, first the Captain's, then the Admiral's, both slightly raised in emphasis. Nicoll was evidently arguing the case for immediate dispersal as ordered; Mayhew heard him saying they should leave now and zigzag. (Once that decision was taken, as Mayhew knew, Nicoll would assume sole mastery of his fate and that of the *Benares* and her complement.) But Mackinnon, sounding peeved, according to Mayhew, demurred.

'No,' Mayhew heard him say. 'We won't do that. We'll wait until midnight.'

'Why can't we get off on our own right now?' asked Nicoll.

'We'll wait until the hours of darkness,' answered Mackinnon, 'we'll have a better chance then.'

After collecting the greatcoat, the 19-year-old Mayhew told Bartlett: 'The Admiral and the Skipper's been having a few words down there.'

'What about?'

'The speed we're doing. The captain wants to get cracking, to get off on our own. The Admiral says no, we'll have a better chance in the dark.'

'You'd better keep that to yourself,' said Bartlett, adding: 'I only hope he's right.'

Second Engineer John McGlashan, who had stood by the ship in Glasgow when she was built and sailed in her ever since, couldn't understand it. 'Why don't we cut and run for it?' he asked Chief Engineer Alex Macauley. The Chief shrugged his shoulders; he didn't know.

Mackinnon had been warned by *Winchelsea* before she departed that a U-boat was operating somewhere ahead of him, beyond 20 degrees West, and this may have influenced his thinking; he would pass through that longitude during the day. He was the man on the spot, and it was his privilege and indeed his job to disregard his instructions if he thought fit. This was Navy tradition. Other factors to take into account included the sea conditions. Winds of Force 5 were blowing and there was a heavy swell, making a submerged attack unlikely and perhaps impossible, periscope viewing being at best intermittent. What danger there was lay in an attack from a submarine on the surface; but visibility was otherwise good, and before any foolhardy U-boat commander could get close enough to the wing of the convoy the look-outs would see him. The *Benares*, and other ships in the convoy, could then use their guns.

Aft of the convoy, in the Western Approaches, U-boats were congregating around HX 71. This incoming convoy was a far greater threat to Germany than an outgoing convoy in ballast, and with the signing of the Lease–Lend agreement a fortnight earlier, the threat was immediate. A destroyer – not *Winchelsea* – attacked a U-boat that afternoon after one ship in the convoy from Halifax was sunk, and soon afterwards *Winchelsea*, having closed HX 71 some time earlier, was ordered by C.-in-C. Western Approaches to attack another enemy submarine in the vicinity. Thus Mackinnon's belief that most of the action lay astern was well founded.

At 18.30 the rain stopped, the sun shone briefly, and a succession of rainbows was pointed out ecstatically by the children. Their powers of recovery were such that at the end of what had for the most part been a miserable day they went to bed deliriously happy. Surely it would be a fine day tomorrow. But as night fell the ship's officers remained apprehensive. Unknown to the passengers, adults and children alike, Western Approaches, in their periodic estimates of U-boat dispositions culled from their intercept service, were signalling: 'One probably still far out in the Atlantic west of 20 degrees West, probably between 57 and 59 degrees North.'

All these warnings were picked up by the radio operators – Alistair Fairweather and his deputy, Canadian John Lazarus – on the *Benares*. They did not constitute a definite sighting, but they did not encourage complacency. The weather remained clear for a time, with a fast-moving cloud-rack and an intermittent moon, but during the evening the wind rose to Force 6, with squalls of gale intensity, accompanied by hailstorms and rain and a confused sea. The station-keeping of outside and stern vessels, especially those that were lightly loaded, was visibly affected, and in these circumstances the worst hazard resulting from keeping the convoy together – with every ship punctiliously blacked out – seemed likely to be collision. At 21.00 Mackinnon ordered zigzagging to cease as it had become too dangerous, but he still gave no order to scatter. He evidently calculated that his plan to disperse at midnight would give each ship several hours of darkness in which to alter course as required by individual destinations and get clear of the scene and each other.

The third and fourth officers, W. J. Lee and Ronald Cooper, both in their early twenties, were on the bridge, with Quartermaster Collin at the wheel. On look-out with them were Apprentice Dennis Haffner and a second quartermaster. Also on the bridge or thereabouts were two of Mayhew's signalman colleagues, Micky Goy and Ernie Charnock, and the chief yeoman. Seaman gunner Harry Peard was on duty on the gun platform aft, and two of the Lascars were also on look-out, one on the forecastle head and one in the crow's nest. The captain and commodore were keeping close at hand, either in the captain's room or the chart room.

If Mackinnon had any qualms about the next three hours he did not express them. The sea conditions seemed totally inimical to U-boat attack.

Four days earlier, when OB 213 sailed from Liverpool, Goering was hoping for a period of favourable weather in which to launch the massed formations of bombers and fighters which he believed would finally destroy the RAF in a decisive victory, leaving the way clear for Operation Sea-Lion, the invasion of Britain. This had to come within the next fortnight, to be reasonably sure of the right sea and weather conditions, or not at all – at least that year. Then on 15 September had come the RAF's greatest day, and although confirmed German losses were actually no more than fifty-six, they were still too many for the *Luftwaffe* to bear. The air battles that day proved quite as decisive as Goering had anticipated, but in the reverse sense. Two days later, on Tuesday, 17 September, as the

City of Benares ploughed ponderously on at half-speed, Admiral Raeder, Chief of the German Naval Staff, was dictating to his War Diary: 'The enemy air force is by no means defeated. On the contrary, it shows increasing activity. The Führer therefore decides to postpone Sea-Lion indefinitely.'

The spur that, with parental concurrence, had driven the majority of the evacuee children from Britain had been blunted. But even if the contents of Raeder's diary had somehow become general knowledge, it was too late to turn back now.

Had Mackinnon dispersed the convoy promptly at noon and set course at speed on his own, it is likely that the *City of Benares* would have escaped. Two minutes after midday Kapitänleutnant Heinrich Bleichrodt, commander of *U48*, sighted the convoy from his conning tower and noted the sizeable passenger liner centre front, so even if the dispersal order had already been given he must have seen her; but it is unlikely he would have caught her. The convoy was zigzagging, but Bleichrodt estimated its mean heading with fair accuracy as west-south-west, about 240 degrees, speed 7 knots.

Bleichrodt was thirty, and this was his first patrol in command of *U48*; he had been appointed two months earlier. Small in stature but squarely built, he was not unlike Captain Nicoll in physique, but in temperament he was outgoing and gregarious, a hard drinker who liked to mix with his contemporaries and enjoyed his leisure. His reputation was for ebullience and friendly good-nature, but friendliness didn't come into his calculations now. With Gunter Prien and others like him he had transferred to the submarine service from the merchant navy in 1932. Leaving his base at Lorient on 5 September, he had begun his patrol in dashing style by sinking three ships in Convoy

SC 3 off north-west Ireland, in the vicinity of 15 degrees West; two were steamers and the third was one of the escorts. *U48* was a Type VIIB boat, displacing 753 tons; a foray deeper into the Atlantic was well within its cruise potential, and 20 degrees West and beyond, especially in the absence of escorts, was a fruitful area of attack.

How was it that Bleichrodt allowed more than nine hours to elapse before making a pass at OB 213, while Mackinnon too procrastinated? The answer was that Mackinnon had guessed right about the swell: submerged attack in daylight would be impossible in these seas. But Bleichrodt was a patient man, prepared to keep up with the convoy at a discreet distance on the surface (he could not have made 7 knots submerged) and wait for the cover of darkness.

On the *Benares*, three of the children's escorts – Marjorie Day, Mary Cornish, and Sybil Gilliat-Smith – lingered over coffee that evening before going up on deck for a breath of fresh air after a day spent mainly in the public rooms or below. The moon, although intermittent, was nearly full, and on either wing they could just discern the blacked-out shapes of other vessels, comforting in their proximity. Initial concern at the departure of the naval escort had evaporated; they had accepted that they were out of the danger zone. The children, under the influence of good food and a regular routine, with plenty of rest, had mostly shaken off home- and seasickness and were bursting with health. Their energy had exhausted the three escorts, and they were glad of a chance to relax. When they went to their cabins after their turn on deck they had no idea that, at the very moment when passengers and crew alike, with a few notable exceptions, were congratulating themselves that the worst of the voyage was over, 600 miles out from the Irish coast and approaching mid-Atlantic, they were moving closer each moment to danger.

Bleichrodt chose to develop his attack from ahead on the port bow, which would give him a clear view of the liner and an uninterrupted run for his torpedo. He had selected his target many hours earlier; he had no hesitation in going for the most distinguished ship by appearance, position and tonnage. Whether or not enemy surveillance had identified the *Benares* as a ship carrying child evacuees and refugees from Nazi persecution, no specific alert seems to have reached *U48*. Bleichrodt judged her to be a passenger ship of about 12,000 tons, a juicy target whatever her cargo, though he would naturally expect it to be something of value. Whatever the ruling might be under international law, German battle instructions were clear. 'Fighting methods will never fail to be employed merely because some international regulations are opposed to them.' Bleichrodt was under no restrictions from Naval High Command about sinking enemy passenger vessels without warning, nor were such vessels protected by any western limit of operations. In any case, when ships were sailing in convoy they were presumed to be forcibly resisting visit and search and were therefore liable to be sunk on sight. To Bleichrodt, the target he had selected was legitimate prey and it was his duty to sink it.

From his brief experience on this his first and uncompleted patrol he judged the target he had chosen to be the commodore ship. Nothing panicked a convoy more than the loss of its leader. There would be further pickings to come.

Mackinnon's belief that no U-boat would attempt to attack in such seas had held good in daylight; it was a mistaken view now. At 22.00 precisely, choosing the right moment as the moon illuminated his target, Bleichrodt fired two bow tubes at the liner heading the convoy.

It was now the German's turn to be mistaken. He had overestimated his angle on the bow, and both torpedoes missed.

Visibility was still good, but none of the look-outs on the *City of Benares*, or anywhere else in the convoy, spotted the torpedo tracks. Thus the convoy steamed unsuspectingly on. Unknown to Mackinnon and everyone else, the *Benares* had had a miraculous escape. But Bleichrodt was not a man to be disheartened by initial failure, and it seemed that his presence was still undiscovered. Altering course briefly in the direction of the head of the convoy, he fired a third torpedo one minute later at the same target.

The torpedo ran for one second short of two minutes before striking the passenger liner somewhere aft and exploding. The ship rocked to its rivets, and in some sections the lighting faltered and failed. From the distress signal that followed, Bleichrodt learned that he had torpedoed the *City of Benares*. Reference to *Lloyd's Register of Shipping* disclosed that she was a vessel of 11,081 tons, well worth the expenditure of three torpedoes whatever her cargo. He had no notion of the human catastrophe he had set in train.

Captain Nicoll, however, saw the implications all too starkly. Relieving Third Officer Lee immediately and sending him and Cooper to their action stations, he set the alarm bells ringing. The ship was already down by the stern and beginning to list. Nicoll thought she might sink within minutes. The launching of lifeboats from a listing ship in tempestuous seas was a nightmare all seamen prayed they would not have to face. With women and children on board it was a ghastly prospect.

The *Benares* was in the open Atlantic, more than 600 miles from the nearest shore, and her escort had departed twenty-one hours earlier. The nearest escorted convoy, by Nicoll's estimate, could not be much less than 300 miles distant, and unless there was some other warship in the vicinity it would be many hours before rescue could come. It seemed inconceivable that help would not be at hand for the children, but Nicoll could not think where it would come from.

Through the darkness the shocked passengers, some in public rooms, some on deck, some preparing for bed, tried to get a glimpse of what was happening. The dim silhouettes of adjacent vessels were still visible. If their ship sank, they told themselves, one of these vessels

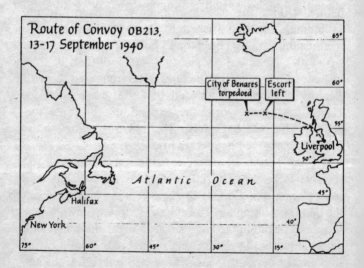

Route of Convoy OB213, 13-17 September 1940

City of Benares torpedoed

Escort left

Liverpool

Atlantic Ocean

Halifax

New York

would pick them up. No one doubted it. This had been the clear understanding of CORB officials, and it seemed obvious to all the passengers, adults and children alike, that this was why the convoy had kept together since the escort left. But the ship's officers must have known to a man that this was not so.

Accompanying vessels were under strict orders from the Admiralty not to attempt rescue work, once their escort had left, if it involved risk to themselves. And risk there would certainly be.

Whether deliberately or through an oversight, these orders had not been countermanded or varied to take account of the exceptional cargo of the *Benares*. When, four minutes after Bleichrodt's third torpedo penetrated No. 5 Hold on the port side aft, a second vessel, the freighter *Marina*, was hit, passengers on the *Benares* watched in horrified disbelief as, on a pyrotechnic signal fired from their own ship's bridge, the convoy scattered.

2

The Good News and the Bad News

The evacuation of non-essential civilians from areas believed to be specially vulnerable to air attack had become government policy in Britain in the mid-1930s, and by 1939 the policy had crystallized into plans for the voluntary exodus, in the event of war, of more than 4 million people, mostly schoolchildren and mothers with younger children. Under the government scheme they were to be billeted in what were thought to be safe areas. The motivation was the rise of Hitler, and particularly the threat of Nazi air power: governments tended to exaggerate its potential for devastation and to underestimate the resilience of civilian populations subjected to it. Indeed the declared object of the British government was not only 'to prevent avoidable loss of life' but also 'to lessen the danger of panic and wild stampeding'. On Friday, 1 September 1939, when war became certain on the German invasion of Poland (whose frontiers Britain and France had guaranteed), complex arrangements for the transport and billeting of the first 1½ million were set in motion.

Simultaneously, sections of the population who enjoyed both mobility and access to private accommodation in safe areas were making their own arrangements for escaping the expected holocaust.

During the anti-climax of the 'Phoney War' that followed, there were no incidents likely to cause panic, still less 'wild stampeding'; if there was any stampede at all it was an exodus in reverse as disillusioned and homesick children drifted back to their parents in the cities and ports. Expectations, when France crumbled and Britain was exposed to the threat of invasion, that there would be a renewed exodus, even perhaps the egregious wild stampede, proved similarly false, only a quarter of the children who should have gone actually going. Families who had been ready to make sacrifices and to split up to give the children a chance of escaping the horrors of aerial bombardment found their sense of unity rekindled by the prospect of being overrun by an invading army. This was a crisis that many families preferred to face together.

To this natural human reaction there was one sharp contradiction, surprising the government and catching them unawares. Parents who had become more than ever possessive of their children in the light of possible invasion were tempted by the visions of a new life for them totally removed from the ravages of war: there was a chance, it seemed, that they might find refuge overseas, in the Dominions or America. Such a glittering prospect had hitherto been available only to those who could afford to pay; how could less well-to-do parents now deny their offspring such an opportunity?

Defeat in France, culminating in the evacuation at Dunkirk, brought a flood of spontaneous offers from private homes in Canada anxious to give sanctuary to British children, and similar offers flowed in from the other Dominions and the United States. By early June some 10,000 such offers had been received through the Canadian government alone, and on the 7th the British government set up an inter-departmental committee under Geoffrey Shakespeare, National Liberal MP for Norwich and Under-Secretary of State for the Dominions, to consider these offers.

Shakespeare, tall and aquiline, was a barrister, a career

politician and a part-time journalist who as a young man had been a protégé of and private secretary to Lloyd George; he was now forty-seven. A family man himself, his initial reaction to the scheme was lukewarm if not actually hostile: as the danger to Britain increased, so, he felt, should the tenacity of her citizens. But he soon came to accept that the task of turning Britain into a fortress would be eased by the evacuation of weaker elements. If this meant an involuntary gift of safety to a selected few, it did not offend his liberal convictions.

The terms of reference of Shakespeare's committee were: 'To consider offers received from overseas to house and care for children, accompanied or unaccompanied, from the European war zone, and to make recommendations thereon.' Five days later Shakespeare reported that two meetings had been held and a third was about to take place, close touch was being maintained with Dominions' governments, and His Majesty's government were confident that it should be possible to devise a practical scheme. But his final phrase was by far the most significant: '*The transport of the children in safety was the crux of the whole matter.*'

On Monday, 17 June Shakespeare presented his report to the War Cabinet, but he had scarcely done so when a messenger arrived with a note for Churchill: France was capitulating. All else at that meeting was inevitably eclipsed by this news, and such discussion as took place about Shakespeare's report appears to have been sketchy. Although the Cabinet minutes recorded the endorsement of the Children's Overseas Reception Scheme, Churchill himself, in Shakespeare's view, was so preoccupied that he did not realize any decision had been taken. Had he done so it seems certain, from his subsequent hostility, that he would have opposed it. At best,

Churchill may be said to have acquiesced in a moment of aberration; at worst, a major Cabinet decision was pushed through while the Prime Minister was nodding.

The next day Clement Attlee, the Lord Privy Seal, deputizing for Churchill, told the House of Commons that the government 'considered the establishment of the necessary machinery for the operation of the scheme to be a matter of the utmost urgency', and a Children's Overseas Reception Board (CORB, already referred to), under the chairmanship of Geoffrey Shakespeare, was established, with a staff accommodated in part of the premises of Thomas Cook and Sons in Berkeley Street. At ten o'clock on the morning of 20 June, the day the CORB offices opened, every corridor inside the building was packed with parents requesting information or waiting for interviews, and nearly 3,000 more were lined up outside the building in a queue hundreds of yards long. The wild stampede that the government had feared earlier had arrived.

Foremost among those who believed that the scheme might become an embarrassment was Churchill himself; awake now to its implications, or anyway to some of them, he deprecated any mass exodus of children because of the impression it might give, real or imagined, of a weakening of national morale. Consequently, Shakespeare that same day issued a warning. Details of the scheme, he said, had not been fully agreed, and in any case its scope was limited by two factors: first, the number of offers received from overseas, and second, the availability of suitable shipping. Any idea of mass migration was absolutely contrary to the wishes of the governments concerned. All that was intended was a safe refuge for a limited number of children, to be achieved according to a well-ordered plan. The overseas evacuation of many thousands was outside the practical bounds of the scheme. But having spelt that out, Shakespeare ended on an optimistic note: the first ships carrying evacuee children – seavacuees, as they came to be known – might be expected to sail in two to three weeks.

Adequate provision for the safety of children during the voyage was to be the subject of discussion between the Admiralty and the Ministry of Shipping. But it was accepted on all sides that there might be losses. 'It will be appreciated,' said The *Times Educational Supplement*, 'that owing to the unprincipled manner in which the enemy conducts warfare certain risks must attend travel by sea; but these must of course be set against the risks of attacks upon this country.' Here in a nutshell lay the parents' dilemma – how to evaluate the opposing risks.

On Sunday evening, 23 June, in a BBC radio broadcast, Shakespeare outlined the CORB scheme in detail, making an effort to weigh up the pros and cons. The preparation of his broadcast must have given him and his staff severe pangs of conscience, as the text emerged rather in the style of one of those comical recitals which fluctuate between the good news and the bad. Children eligible were those over five and under sixteen, and Dominion governments were currently ready to welcome 20,000 as a beginning; but there was the limiting factor of shipping. Talk of hundreds of thousands of children escaping overseas was dangerous and stupid; but he expected the first parties to sail fairly soon. There would be steady outgoings thereafter; but no mass migration. It would be an orderly affair, well planned and executed, with special escorts, plus doctors and nurses, appointed to look after the children; but he would not counsel parents on what was best for their children: 'That is advice I cannot give.' The government thought it right to provide the facilities –

notwithstanding the difficulties to be overcome and the risks of the voyage. Finally:

'You have to weigh the danger to which your child is exposed in this country, whether by invasion or air raids, against the risks to which every ship that leaves these shores is subjected in wartime by enemy action, whether by air, submarine or mine. The risks of the voyage are obvious and the choice is one for which you alone are responsible.' The buck was passed to the parents.

Shakespeare then gave details of how parents should apply: for children from the grant-aided schools, to the local education authority; for children from the fee-paying schools, direct to CORB. There were separate arrangements for Scotland.

Parents listening to the broadcast up to this point, hoping to have their minds made up for them, must have felt thoroughly confused by Shakespeare's guarded and woolly attempt to present a balanced picture. Shakespeare himself seems to have felt that he had possibly undersold the scheme, putting parents off, as he had another go at presenting the scheme in a more positive light. 'I know there will be much burning of heart at the thought of parting, but parents will not allow themselves to be influenced by selfish considerations where they believe the safety of their children is concerned.' Even this, although not intended to be ambiguous, was capable of more than one interpretation.

Whatever the effect of the broadcast, applications soon exceeded capacity, rising rapidly to 20,000 a day. Of these applications 74 per cent were for children from grant-aided schools, designated by CORB as coming from 'working-class' families. One in every seven applications was for the United States of America, although America for the moment was outside the CORB scheme.

Having based their calculations on the increasing reluctance of parents to evacuate their children within the United Kingdom and the vast numbers that had returned to the cities in recent months, the government, trying to cope with over 211,000 applications in the space of ten days for a possible 20,000 places, were obliged on 4 July to announce that no further requests could be handled.

On the same day, news came of an incident which had immediate repercussions on the new scheme: a fast unescorted liner, of a kind strongly favoured by CORB for transporting children to Canada – the *Arandora Star* – was torpedoed and sunk in the Atlantic, with heavy loss of life. This convinced the Admiralty and the Ministry of Shipping, who bore the responsibility, that the safest method of transporting the children was in convoy, a view they promptly urged on the government despite representations by CORB, Shakespeare seeing in this ruling a mortal threat to his scheme.

The preoccupation of escort vessels and other antisubmarine craft with successive Allied withdrawals from the continent of Europe, culminating in the enforced neutrality of the French fleet, were only the most immediate of the Navy's problems. Added to them were the extension of hostilities to the Mediterranean area with Italy's entry into the war, the withdrawal in early July of American shipping from belligerent ports and seas, and, finally, the threat of invasion. The Navy's resources were so overstrained that a reappraisal of all escort duties became essential. On 10 July the War Cabinet, accepting that warships could not be taken off anti-invasion tasks to provide escorts, declared the CORB scheme to be in abeyance. 'The heavier tasks now falling on the Navy have clearly made it less easy to provide the escort of warships necessary for the safe transport of children across the sea,' the government announced.

Here for the first time the government was declaring the policy that ships carrying evacuee children must be escorted by warships. 'The chief difficulty is not shipping,' said Attlee, 'but the shortage of naval vessels to convoy them.' He blamed the radical change in Britain's position specifically on the withdrawal of the French fleet from the conflict and added: 'In view of the fate of the *Arandora Star* the government cannot take the responsibility of sending shiploads of children except in convoy.'

Permits for children travelling at private expense, however, were still being granted, so long as parents accepted the risks. Some of these children were going to family friends, others were the children of professional men whose opposite numbers in the States had got together and issued a block invitation. Such children came from parallel backgrounds, on the approximate cultural level of their hosts. But the CORB scheme was directed chiefly – though not exclusively – at children from the state-aided schools, and its postponement rankled. The fact that many thousands of children of professional people had not only gone but were still going, whereas six weeks after the CORB scheme's inception only a handful of eligible children had been transported, was seen as an outrage, one law for the rich and another for the poor. Labour MPs voiced their suspicion that the entire official scheme had been a pretence and a camouflage, to be cancelled at the first opportunity. Attlee was asked in the House: 'Is the right honourable gentleman aware that it is commonly held in the country that now some thousands of rich people's children had gone overseas there was to be no opportunity for the children in elementary schools?'

The whole purpose of the government scheme, replied

Attlee, deputizing for Churchill, was that there should be a proper proportion of children from the elementary schools. This had never been spelt out in so many words before. Shakespeare for his part denied that the scheme had been mere window-dressing. It had been government policy endorsed by the War Cabinet and supported almost unanimously in the House and, he thought, in the country. The scheme was non-discriminatory and applied without regard to parents' circumstances. That was its object. The current hiatus was not a cancellation but a genuine postponement. As soon as the escort situation improved the scheme would be reactivated.

Doubts of the government's good faith were also expressed in the House of Lords. What steps were the government taking, it was demanded, to ensure that children from state-aided schools were given equal opportunities with children of the well-to-do to accept the many generous offers from abroad? Reiterating that the scheme was in abeyance, not abandoned, and rejecting accusations of favouritism, the government pointed again to the governing factor – shortage of shipping. Admitting that the demand for places had greatly exceeded expectations, they emphasized yet again the dependence of the scheme on the availability of escort vessels and their refusal to send children overseas except in convoy. As for the many privately booked children who had gone already, surely it wasn't suggested that the government should have stopped them?

To this question, intended to be rhetorical, the member for Llanelly, Jim Griffiths (Labour) gave a categoric answer. If the government scheme was impracticable, for whatever reason, it would be far better to abandon it, for the time being anyway. That being so, the government ought not to help, indeed ought actually to prevent, any children of well-to-do parents from leaving the country.

This smacked of levelling down, rather than the levelling up that the CORB scheme aimed to achieve. But Griffiths felt an understandable indignation at the sight of pictures of children of the moneyed classes enjoying safe and comfortable surroundings in America and elsewhere while the CORB children languished, and he complained bitterly that class distinction at such a time had a bad effect on the nation's morale. It was a people's war, and the fact that certain people had got their children away in advance of the government scheme had a bad psychological effect.

Dissatisfaction and disillusion were not confined to the eastern side of the Atlantic. Lord Lothian, the British Ambassador in Washington, recording the great disappointment felt in America at the postponement, warned that all the work done by voluntary organizations was being undermined. Throughout the United States the prospect of giving a home and shelter to evacuated European children had evoked tremendous interest and enthusiasm, and a Gallup Poll had found half a million American homes ready to take British children. Numerous committees had been formed to operate schemes, the most influential being the United States Committee for the Care of European Children, set up by the US government, with Eleanor Roosevelt as honorary president (she attended committee meetings) and Marshall Field as chairman. Local sub-committees were formed all over the States, substantial funds were raised and the names of prospective foster parents collected, while a parallel committee operated in London. What Lord Lothian feared was that lukewarm support from the British government might cause the Americans to lose interest.

Lothian believed that if the British government made its gratitude to the American public for its generous offers abundantly clear, and confirmed that shortage of shipping was the only reason for postponement, there would be a spontaneous demand in America for the actual task of transporting the children to be undertaken by the United States under a safe-conduct agreement; Marshall Field's committee was already working on this. Meanwhile, to counteract the general impression that only rich children were being transported, Field's committee offered to pay the passage of 100 poor children by Cunarder to New York provided that they travelled at their parents' risk and provided that the British government guaranteed to repatriate them after the war.

In their reply the Foreign Office gave Lord Lothian the expression of gratitude he had asked for, and they explained that the difficulty was not a shortage of shipping but the strong responsibility that rested on the government to see that any children who went overseas under the government scheme were given such naval protection as would reasonably ensure their safety during the voyage. Reminding the ambassador of the fate of the *Arandora Star*, they added: 'In present circumstances it is essential to concentrate our whole naval forces on the task of meeting overriding demands of national security. It is this consideration alone which has forced the government reluctantly to the conclusion that they must postpone operation of the scheme until the situation at sea enables them to provide naval escort for ships employed for this purpose.'

Before the postponement, CORB had been planning, as a start, to send an initial batch of 150 children to Canada, followed by two larger groups of 750 each. Meanwhile, under schemes totally outside the influence of CORB, 2,000 children were to pass through Canada on their way to the United States. This was seen in Canada, where channels for accepting 10,000 children were fully organized and waiting, as an affront, and those concerned pronounced themselves hurt and discouraged. Foreseeing strife in American schools when British children found themselves alongside children of German, Italian and Irish descent, the High Commissioner for Canada pointed out that no problems of this nature would face the children in Canada.

Spontaneous, generous-hearted and disinterested sympathy for Britain's children was in danger of developing into unseemly competition, and it was at this point that Winston Churchill delivered himself, in the House and on paper, of opinions on the CORB scheme which poured further troubled waters on the oil dispensed by the Foreign Office. His attitude, even before the scheme was first mooted, had been that he abhorred anything likely to weaken confidence at a time 'when all must brace themselves for the supreme struggle' (24 May). Now, on 18 July, he declared: 'It is most undesirable that anything in the nature of a large-scale exodus from this country should take place, and I do not believe the military situation requires or justifies such a proceeding, having regard to the relative dangers of staying and going.' After confirming that the official scheme was postponed rather than abandoned, he added: 'I must frankly admit that the full bearings of this question were not appreciated by the British government at the time it was first raised.' He may well have meant 'not appreciated by me'. But in all this he was fully supported by Attlee.

Solidarity within the Commonwealth, and the active sympathy and help of the United States, were desired by Churchill no less than by others, but he was thoroughly piqued at being caught on the hop by the CORB scheme. When the Home Secretary, Sir John Anderson, asked him for some expression of Britain's gratitude to be delivered to Canadian Prime Minister Mackenzie King when the first party sailed, perhaps by hand of the senior child, Churchill replied bluntly: 'I certainly do not propose to send a message by the senior child to Mr Mackenzie King, or by the junior child either. If I sent a message by anyone, it would be that I entirely deprecate any stampede from this country at the present time.'

Another point of view, also disapproving in tone, was put by the Headmaster of Winchester College in a letter to *The Times*.

It cannot be right [he argued] to encourage these boys and girls to think first of their own safety and security. It may be possible for them to help here in many ways. How can we with any consistency continue to speak of training in citizenship and in leadership while at the same time we arrange for them against their will to leave the post of danger? . . . I believe it is our duty to encourage those for whom we are responsible to stand fast and carry on.

In the main the CORB children were not, of course, leaving against their will. Nor were they thinking first of their own safety and security. The notion of being sunk in mid-Atlantic certainly occurred to them, but it held more possibilities of adventure than being bombed or invaded, and it was adventure that attracted them. The rescue that would certainly follow, and a new life in Canada, was all part of the fun. Only a few of the more mature children feared the voyage or saw their projected departure as in any way cowardly.

Churchill's statement of 18 July clearly implied that it was safer for children to stay where they were. But he interfered no further than that. Parents of children already registered under the CORB scheme had made their decision, many of them were under pressure from relatives overseas who were pleading for the children to be sent, and there is no evidence of so much as a token withdrawal of the 211,000 applications on the files following Churchill's deprecatory remarks.

Circumventing the escort problem by employing American ships under a guarantee of safe passage from the belligerents, as suggested by Marshall Field's committee, had meanwhile found favour with the US government, and they put an appropriate Bill before the House of Representatives and got it approved during August. But the Bill evoked no enthusiasm from the British government, whose policy was to ask no favours, and who feared that the Germans would demand from the US government, and perhaps obtain, some concession in return. Also a gesture by Germany to allow a limited number of British children and child refugees from Europe to cross the Atlantic unmolested would suggest a degree of humanity which might increase respect for the Nazis and reduce sympathy for Britain. As it happened, however, an approach by the American government was turned down by the German High Command, as captured documents confirm: 'Germany must most decidedly reject every request referring to this matter . . . It is entirely contrary to our interests if the power of resistance of the British people is strengthened by the evacuation of children and refugees.' The British government, believing that the Nazis had missed what might have proved a useful propaganda coup, actually welcomed the rejection.

Hitler's orders to the German Navy when the war started were to wage war in accordance with the Prize Regulations then in force under international treaty. His orders were not issued in any pacific spirit, but in the hope that the swift overrunning of Poland would coerce Britain and France into suing for peace. (The sinking of the *Athenia* on the first day of the war, which convinced the British that unrestricted submarine warfare had started, was actually an error by the U-boat commander.) But as soon as it became apparent to Hitler that his hopes were in vain, he began the progressive removal of restrictions previously agreed. As early as 23 September 1939, orders were issued that all merchant ships making use of their wireless on being stopped by U-boats were to be sunk or taken in prize; this marked a significant step towards unrestricted sea warfare. Before September was out, 150,000 tons of British shipping had been sunk.

The month of October brought further escalation. On 2 October the German Navy was granted complete freedom to attack darkened ships, whatever their nationality, off the British and French coasts. On the 4th, observance of the Prize Regulations was cancelled in the Atlantic as far out as 15 degrees West, and this was extended to 20 degrees West a fortnight later. On the 17th, permission was given to attack without warning all ships identified as hostile. A month later it was confirmed that passenger liners were included in this instruction, though they were granted the distinction of having to be *clearly* identified as hostile.

Unfortunately, the illegality of many of these orders was not as clear-cut as might be imagined. Article 22 of the London Naval Treaty of 1930 – to which the signatories were the United States, Great Britain, France, Italy and Japan – was carried forward, when the treaty expired, into a Protocol signed in London by the United States and Britain on 6 November 1936; provision was written into it for the subsequent accession of other states. Germany acceded in the same year and Russia in 1937. According to the Protocol, unless a merchantman persistently refused to stop on being summoned, or actively resisted visit or search, it must not be sunk or rendered incapable of navigation until its crew, passengers and ship's papers had been put in a place of safety – which meant either being taken aboard another vessel or being provided with lifeboats for its entire complement and assured of safe weather conditions and the proximity of land. With the introduction of radar, improved radio communications and long-range air patrols, obedience to these instructions would have exposed U-boats to counter-attack so frequently as to seriously inhibit their operations. However, Article 22 allowed that the rescue of survivors need not be an absolute priority if it endangered the safety of the mission of the vessel which carried out the sinking, and this was bound to be interpreted by submarine commanders as a licence to do as they pleased. As noted by John and Ann Tusa in their account of the Nuremberg Trials, 'scrupulous attention to the rules of giving warning of attack and help to survivors was clearly in conflict with those aspects of the law which allowed considerations of one's own safety'.[1] To a U-boat commander, all shipping, whether naval, merchant or neutral, crippled or sinking, and all maritime air operations, were a potential danger.

Rules for the conduct of sea warfare that were intended to be binding were thus rendered insubstantial, and Britain's unique vulnerability, as an island dependent for survival on supplies from overseas, rendered her denunciations of this form of warfare sophistical, much as did the later denunciations by the Nazis of the Allied bombing offensive. It was simply another form of modern warfare that had to be defeated if eventual victory was to be won. Ironically, in defending themselves as best they could by arming their merchantmen and sailing them in convoy, Britain deprived them of their presupposed and, as it

---

[1] *The Nuremberg Trial*, by Ann and John Tusa (Macmillan, 1983)

turned out, wholly illusory legal protection. Who broke the rules first was academic: it needed no great casuistry on the part of the Nazis to argue that their submarines were legitimately attacking 'armed merchant cruisers'.

In the first six months of 1940 the U-boats were relatively inactive, although they were successful enough for Churchill, in the course of a bitter attack on this form of warfare in a broadcast on 31 March while he was still First Lord of the Admiralty, to stress the damage being inflicted on Allied shipping. He went on to praise the convoy system: 'Only one in 800 neutral ships which have resorted to our protection has been sunk.' Outside the shelter of the Allied navies, however, as he declaimed with typical incisiveness, 'merciless, baffled, pent-up spite has been wreaked upon all who come within the Nazi clutch'.

By June the U-boats were back on the Atlantic trade routes in force. Operating now from captured bases on the Bay of Biscay, they were able to extend their range to 600 miles and more out into the Atlantic. By early August Churchill was writing to his successor at the Admiralty, A. V. Alexander, and the First Sea Lord, Admiral Sir Dudley Pound: 'The repeated severe losses in the North-West Approaches are most grievous, and I wish to be assured that they are being grappled with . . . There seems to have been a great falling off in the control of these Approaches.' Conceding that this was largely due to the shortage of destroyers through invasion precautions, he demanded 'a great new impulse' to counteract the threat. Yet on the whole the convoy system was serving Britain well. Publishing a picture taken from an escorting warship of a convoy at sea, *The Times*, on 12 July, said that the latest returns showed that of the many thousands of ships convoyed only forty had been lost since the war began.

Instructions to parents of selected children were meanwhile being issued by CORB in anticipation of the lifting of the ban. Parents were informed that their children had been accepted for evacuation subject to medical examination, though this did not mean they would necessarily be sailing at an early date. 'You may have heard over the wireless,' said the letter, 'or have read in the Press, that the government cannot take responsibility for sending children overseas under the Scheme without adequate naval protection.' Parents were further advised that when they did eventually hear, as shipping accommodation became available, that their offspring had been brought forward from the waiting lists, they could conclude 'that the ship in which your child (children) is (are) to sail will be convoyed. If at the very last moment there were a sudden change in the situation and the Admiralty informed the Board that the ship could not, after all, be convoyed, *the arrangements for sailing would be cancelled forthwith* and you would be duly notified.'[2] Parents felt they could have nothing more explicit than that.

What constituted adequate protection was something they were happy to leave to the Navy. But implicit was the definition of the word convoy: it meant, to them – and *The Times* was not the only newspaper which published an impressive picture of such an aggregation – a group of merchant ships protected by naval escort. They did not know, and they were not told, that such destroyers, sloops and corvettes as were available lacked the endurance to take them farther west than a so-called 'limit of convoy' of 17 degrees West, 300 miles off the north-west Irish

[2] CORB's italics

coast. Nor were they told that this distance, far from overlapping U-boat range, fell at least 300 miles short of it.

From the 'limit of convoy' on – again unknown to parents – ships in convoy normally dispersed and proceeded independently, while the escort picked up the next incoming convoy. The sailing of the outgoing convoy was timed to this end. It was a method of operation which, while giving maximum economy and utilization to Britain's overstretched escort forces, advertised the imminent appearance of the one convoy to any U-boat commander in contact with the other. This enabled him to strike at one convoy before the escort arrived and at the other after the escort left.

Parents were under no misapprehension about the utter ruthlessness of submarine warfare, and they had been warned from the first of the dangers. But the letter they received from CORB served only to reassure them. They were given a totally false impression of adequate and uninterrupted protection by the Royal Navy. They were not told that, through no fault of that Service, their confidence was exaggerated and even perhaps mistaken. Risks there were, that much they knew, but they were left in ignorance of their magnitude.

In August the U-boat war intensified still further, and the upward graph of losses reflected the further drain on resources caused by anti-invasion measures. Yet week after week, with the Royal Navy called upon by the Admiralty and the Ministry of Shipping to cope with the vital duties of escort and apparently able to do so, hundreds of CORB children assembled at the ports of embarkation and sailed in convoy for Canada, Australia, New Zealand and South Africa, or semi-officially to the United States. There was no public announcement of the lifting of the ban – which was understandable for security reasons, although the scheme was public knowledge – and no traceable government decision. The suspension was simply terminated, the Admiralty and the Ministry of Shipping now apparently feeling ready to accept the responsibility.

Despite warnings to Shakespeare that he would be advised to tread warily because the policy was unpopular with 'higher authority' – a reference presumably to Churchill – the evacuation went forward apace, and without untoward incident. Credit for this must go to the CORB organization and above all to the Royal Navy, who could scarcely have been any less stretched than before.

Indeed, it is not clear how many obstacles previously attested to were bypassed or overcome. Was judgement clouded, perhaps, by the accusations of class discrimination, or by the threat that goodwill overseas, particularly in America, might be forfeited? Did the project proceed on a tide of inertia, a reluctance to call a halt, while things were going well, to an operation that had raised such extravagant hopes and whose cancellation would be certain to be politically misunderstood? Or was it the fear, as the air battle raged overhead, that soon it might be too late, and that some at least of the children might as well take their chance while they could? Another inducement, so far as the Atlantic was concerned, was that, through the introduction of ships manned by predominantly Asian crews, the requisite passenger accommodation could be made available.

At the Board of Trade it had been agreed with the Seamen's Union some time earlier to extend the geographical limits for the employment of Lascar crews to the North Atlantic; previously they had been restricted to latitudes to which they were more accustomed. The extension substantially enlarged their scope of operations and that of the ships they crewed. The Board of Trade were greatly influenced at the time by the opinions of the marine superintendents of both the P. and O. and Ellerman Lines, who testified strongly that Lascars should not be considered inferior to white crews from the viewpoint of discipline or steadfastness in emergency; although there had been wartime incidents where Lascars had got out of hand, there had been similar falls from grace by European crews. During the summer of 1940, with shipping space under increasing pressure, three ships of Ellerman's City Line, the *City of Benares*, the *City of Simla*, and the *City of Paris*, each with a majority of Lascar crews, were made available for carrying evacuated children to any destination; they were the first Lascar-manned ships to be offered without strings. It was inevitable that doubts of this departure from previous practice should be expressed and racial comparisons made.

At the Ministry of War Transport the testimony of the two marine superintendents was immediately recalled. It was also admitted that if ships with Lascar crews were ruled out, the evacuation of the children would be seriously obstructed. The three Ellerman Line ships were ideally suited to the task, and an eagerness to use them was natural.

There was, in addition, an attendant problem of some sensitivity. However discreetly the issue was handled, a negative decision would soon become known and would be regarded as a slur on the Lascars. It would certainly be resented and might lead to trouble. In the light of these factors, a unanimous conclusion was reached that there was insufficient reason to discriminate against them. Nevertheless it was also felt desirable, again unanimously, that such ships should only be used if others were not available, and that the numbers of children carried in them should be kept as low as possible. This would maintain the flow of seavacuees while avoiding a political row.

For the future, efforts were to be made to ensure that ships with European crews were available; but for the present the employment of the Ellerman ships was to stand. Racial prejudice undoubtedly played a part in this hotchpotch of a compromise. But by the same token, had the children been Asian, it might have been understandable if Asians had preferred Asian crews.

Although the first ships carrying sponsored children across the Atlantic – manned by European crews – got through safely, overall losses showed no diminution, indeed the reverse. There were good reasons for this. Hitler was resolved to intensify the air war and naval blockade against Britain, and in pursuit of this he issued a new directive on 1 August – Directive No. 17 – to take effect as soon as practicable. This required the Naval High Command to plan a total blockade of the British Isles, involving the removal of all remaining restrictions, with particular reference to neutral ships. Within the new blockade area, which was to extend in the North Atlantic to 20 degrees West, U-boats would be free to attack all ships without warning, except for a few specified vessels of the Irish Free State. The coordinates of the extended area were given to neutral countries on 17 August, the Press were informed the next day, and Admiral Karl Doenitz, as Flag Officer U-boats, prepared to execute the new policy from the 21st. While this was inhibiting for neutral countries sympathetic to Britain and trading with her – especially for the United States – it had no bearing on British and Allied ships and convoys, which were already liable to be attacked without warning wherever they might be. The limiting factor for them was the range of U-boats.

An even greater threat to British seaborne trade, and to those charged with responsibility for the safety of vessels carrying evacuee children to Canada, were five sinkings of merchant vessels – one Norwegian and four British – that occurred in a four-day period immediately following the implementation of the new directive. All were sunk by U-boat, all without warning, and all a long way west of 20 degrees West, hitherto regarded as the approximate limit of U-boat activity. They were in fact the first sinkings by U-boat at such a distance from the European mainland. All but one of these vessels, however, was sailing independently, a circumstance from which the Admiralty, and other champions of the convoy system, no doubt derived some comfort. Nevertheless the sinkings marked a significant escalation in the U-boat threat.

The losses were not made public, but they stimulated Churchill into minuting Pound in some perturbation. 'The enclosed returns show losses of over 40,000 tons in a single day. I regard this matter as so serious as to require special consideration by the War Cabinet.' He wanted a full report on causes, measures already taken and measures the Admiralty might propose, to reach him for consideration by the War Cabinet on Thursday, 29 August.

While the War Cabinet were studying the report, the luxury Dutch liner *Volendam* (15,434 tons), formerly plying the Amsterdam–New York route, left Liverpool for Halifax under escort, carrying a total of 606 passengers of whom 321 were sponsored British seavacuees. She had a British master (Captain J. P. Webster), a retired British admiral as convoy commodore and a mainly Dutch crew. Not only was she the commodore ship but, like the *Benares* a fortnight later, she was also the biggest ship in the convoy and the most inviting target. She was carrying a cargo of wheat, to earn Britain much-needed dollars, making her, by any standards, perfectly legitimate prey.

The convoy, like OB 213, was sailing in nine columns, and the *Volendam*, again like the *Benares*, was the leading ship in the fifth or centre column, the focus of the convoy for friend and enemy alike.

Shortly before 22.00 on 30 August, the second day out, a vessel on *Volendam*'s port bow was torpedoed, and at 22.00 precisely the *Volendam* herself was hit and badly holed. A second torpedo, mercifully, failed to explode. The convoy was still under escort, approximately seventy miles off Bloody Foreland, and with the ship listing to port and the weather worsening, Webster decided to transfer his passengers, while this was still practicable, to three ships that were standing by for that purpose. Eighteen lifeboats were successfully launched, without damage thanks to the protection afforded by Schat skids, and all occupants were safely picked up. The only casualty was the purser, who fell between the ship and a lifeboat and was lost. Meanwhile the ship stayed afloat, part of the crew remained on board, and when wind and sea permitted the *Volendam* was taken in tow, arriving off the Clyde to be beached on the morning of 2 September.

The torpedoing of the *Volendam* occurred in the North-Western Approaches, where U-boats had done so much damage that summer. With escort vessels present, it had been reasonably safe, as well as consistent with Admiralty orders, for nearby ships to stop and assist in the work of rescue. An alteration of course had been ordered some time earlier by the Admiralty, so there had been some warning that U-boats were about. But it was gratifying that Captain Webster was afterwards able to report:

As regards the conduct of the passengers and crew, everybody remained calm, there was no panic whatsoever. The children went to their assembly places in perfect order and I must say their conduct was inspiring. I greatly admire the way they behaved. Every member of the crew performed his duty – the engine-room staff, the boat crews, and those detailed to investigate the condition of the ship and report on same. In some boats the children were singing and the whole operation was more like an extensive boat drill than a reality.

This last sentence, perhaps, was the most pertinent: the whole operation had gone like clockwork, as if in an exercise. It was the perfect model for others to copy, and it demonstrated that large numbers of children would respond with admirable coolness in emergency under expert direction. It also confirmed that being torpedoed was a survivable experience. Yet the *Volendam* incident was hardly a true rehearsal of what might happen to a ship torpedoed in mid-Atlantic in gale conditions and afterwards left to its own devices.

321 children had got away with it, and there was great rejoicing on their return to the Clyde. 319 of them were sent back to their homes, to give parents and children time to reconsider; but two for whom any such return was impracticable – Michael Brooker, ten, of Bromley, whose home was threatened by an unexploded bomb, and Patricia Allen, twelve, of Liverpool, similarly homeless – were delivered back to the Sherwood's Lane School at Fazackerley, where they were added to the priority list for the next sailing – which proved to be the *City of Benares*. Patricia Allen professed herself quite unperturbed by her

experience and said she was still greatly looking forward to a new life in Canada.

One child on the *Volendam* took no part in the mass escape: this was a nine-year-old boy who was sound asleep at the time of the torpedoing and got left behind in the darkness and confusion. Waking up during the night, he found himself alone in a silent, empty cabin and, as it seemed, in a silent, empty ship. The nucleus of crewmen and engineers were out of sight. After searching adjacent cabins and finding them deserted he hurried on deck to find davits empty and ropes dangling, with still no one in sight. It seemed clear that he and the ship had been abandoned. This was too much to take in at one go, and as the ship seemed to be floating happily he returned to his cabin and slept soundly till daylight. Exploring the ship next morning, he found a piece of the torpedo casing and commandeered it as a souvenir. He also noticed that there were other ships close by, and discovered he was not quite in sole command of the vessel. Sadly, this charming story was censored by Shakespeare, who intercepted the boy's father in Glasgow and persuaded the family to keep it to themselves. He feared, surely mistakenly, that the confidence of parents would be impaired by its general release.

The exemplary rescue of the *Volendam* children may well have lulled the authorities into a false sense of security; what might have proved a timely warning was interpreted as confirmation that even when torpedoed the children had an excellent chance of escape. The fact that they were spared partly because a second torpedo failed to explode appears to have been overlooked. Had a few young lives been tragically lost, the lesson might have been learnt and a far greater disaster averted.

Again it may be that a pall of inertia paralysed reaction.

Hands had been put to the plough, no one wanted to look back, and some had a vested interest in continuing with the scheme. And the original stimulus remained. On 7 September the blitz started on London, and rows of lifeless children in hospital morgues supplied a tragic reminder of the horrors the seavacuees would be leaving behind. On 10 September, as already recorded, the next batch of sponsored children, their numbers restricted to ninety by the compromise decision, were called forward to Liverpool.

Two months earlier the torpedoing of the unescorted *Arandora Star* had wrung recriminations from the Admiralty and a rigid insistence, on which the government immediately acted, that any further children's ships must be convoyed. There were lessons to be learned from the *Volendam* experience, too, if only in the greater protection that might have been afforded the children by rearranging the convoy's configuration, but no comparable review of tactics was forthcoming. On 13 September the *City of Benares* sailed and acted as commodore ship in the centre front of the convoy, just like the *Volendam*.

3

'Abandon Ship!'

'Fancy – it's happened again!'

For Patricia Allen, from Liverpool, one of the two survivors from the *Volendam* who had been transferred to the *City of Benares*, it was a case of *déjà vu*. The muffled thud and the burgeoning explosion were frighteningly familiar. Eardrums had scarcely recovered from the percussion when the tinkling clatter of glass and crockery and the creak of splintered and shattered woodwork produced an orchestral reprise. The twelve-year-old Patricia reminded herself and others that the *Volendam* hadn't sunk; perhaps the *City of Benares* wouldn't sink either.

Johnny Baker, from Southall, heard the alarm bells clanging and thought it was just another drill. But this sturdy seven-year-old fought his way out of the cocoon in which his bunk bed was made up and ran round waking the others. One of them was his older brother Robert. 'Come on – it's another drill – we've got to move.' The third boy was scrabbling in the darkness for his glasses.

Brixton boy Jack Keeley had gone to bed with the comforting feeling that they were miles away from the war. The relaxation of the order that they must go to bed fully dressed assured him of that. He had been dozing happily, listening to the hypnotic hum of the turbines far below in the bowels of the ship. Then came the explosion.

'We've been torpedoed!'

Derek Capel and Billy Short, the two boys with younger brothers in quarantine on the boat deck, were more dismayed than most. Promises to parents to look after kid brothers were tremulously recalled, but there was nothing they could do about them; their cabin door was jammed and they were trapped. Water was gushing over their feet and for a ghastly moment they thought it was the sea. Then they realized it was coming from a split pipe leading to a hand-basin. A wardrobe had collapsed on them, but in falling away from its housing it provided an avenue of escape. Tearing it from such fixtures as remained, they managed to charge through the gap into the corridor. There they heard their escort, Father O'Sullivan, hammering on an adjacent door. He too was trapped. They tugged and pushed at the door and its handle and somehow got him out. 'Come on, lads,' said O'Sullivan, 'we've got to find our way to Boat 12.'

On the port side, directly above No. 5 Hold, where the torpedo had struck, many of the girls were hurled out of their bunks. Several were bruised and injured, some seriously. The explosion was succeeded by a pungent, sulphurous smell. Beth Cummings sat up in her bunk and stayed there for what seemed a minute, still half asleep, heavy-lidded and bemused. Eventually she jumped out and shouted to the other two girls in her cabin. After groping unsuccessfully for her coat and life-jacket she switched on the light. Nothing happened. The lighting in the children's cabins and the alleyways leading to them had been extinguished by the explosion. This wasn't at all like the routine lifeboat drills, which had all been held in daylight.

Water was seeping round her ankles, again from fractured pipes, and after locating coat and life-jacket she started making her way out of the cabin. Then she realized that the seasick Joan Irving was being left behind. Joan was too weak to do anything for herself and could scarcely walk.

In the next cabin Bess Walder found her exit blocked, but someone who had escaped into the corridor helped to pull her clear. She joined her friend Beth in helping Joan Irving into the corridor, only to find the way forward obstructed by damaged woodwork and other debris.

Senior escort Marjorie Day seized her coat and life-jacket as water flooded into her cabin, collected the CORB doctor, Margaret Zeal, and hurried to the children's quarters through broken glass and fallen furniture. Some of the children were still in their bunks. 'Get up, get up!' she called. Every child she saw had a life-jacket, and one of the ship's nurses was helping a little girl who had been injured. On the starboard side, one boy had been killed in the explosion.

Mary Cornish, trying to reach the children in her care, groped through passageways in the darkness, but at length found her route blocked by the debris that had halted Beth Cummings and her friends. Wrenching aside partitions and kicking and pushing at obstacles, tearing her flesh in the process, she reached the children.

Chief Officer Joe Hetherington, a massive fellow, six feet four inches and barrel-chested, was asleep in his cabin when he was awakened by the violence of the impact and the ringing of the alarms. He went straight to the bridge and reported to Captain Nicoll. 'Go aft and find out the extent of the damage,' said Nicoll. On the way Hetherington noticed that various members of the lifeboat crews, Asian and European, were assembling on the boat deck and awaiting orders.

On reaching the after end of the boat deck Hetherington saw at once that the explosion had wrecked No. 5 Hold. It had thrown off all the beams and hatches from that compartment, also those from No. 4. He soon learned, too, that the force of the detonation had blown in the watertight door in the tunnel leading to the engine-room, and that the engine-room itself was flooding.

Chief Engineer Alex Macauley was reading at his desk prior to his tour of inspection. A bump followed by a tell-tale shudder stopped him in mid-sentence and he rammed his cap on his head and hurried to the engine-room. When he got down to the platform he stepped into water up to his ankles. On duty were the fourth and sixth engineers, and he ordered them to close the main injection valve and open the injection valve for the bilge. At that moment the main telegraph from the bridge rang 'Half-ahead'. The water was now up to Macauley's knees and he immediately rang back 'Stop!'

Leaving the platform to locate the source of the flooding, he found the watertight door in the tunnel had been blasted away. Meanwhile Captain Nicoll was ringing through from the bridge: 'What's the position in the engine-room?'

'We're up to our waists in water.'

'Get everybody out and go to your boat stations.'

By the time Macauley left the platform the water had risen to his chest. It was time to go. At the top of the stairway, where the remote emergency controls were situated, he closed the automatic bulkhead stop valve and opened the emergency vacuum-breaker cock to ensure that the engines would not move again. Then he went up to his cabin on the boat deck, collected his life-jacket, and continued to the emergency dynamo-room. Electrician Jim Swales was there and had got the dynamo started; soon the emergency lights were burning.

Second Engineer John McGlashan had turned in after coming off watch two hours earlier. Pulling a raincoat over his pyjamas, putting on his shoes and grabbing a life-jacket, he too started for the engine-room. He got no farther than the top of the stairway when he met the other engineers coming up. 'Have you stopped the engines?'

'Yes – the engine-room's flooded.'

Hetherington had meanwhile returned to the bridge and reported to Nicoll. The list was no worse but the stern-down angle was increasing, and there was no hope of saving the ship. Thus Nicoll had already given the order: '*Lower the boats to the embarkation deck. Prepare to abandon ship.*'

Hetherington's next thought was the children. Hurrying to their quarters below and astern, he found columns of children, shepherded by their escorts and the nurses recruited by Anderson, heading for their muster stations like school parties visiting a museum. Discipline was complete, and children who had escaped the full force of the explosion were treating the experience as an adventure. But when they got to their muster station, the children's playroom, they staggered back from what had become a jagged precipice. It was directly below this point that the torpedo had struck. Shutting the chasm from their minds, they continued to their boat stations on the same – promenade – deck.

In the dining-room, Purser John Anderson was preparing United States passenger schedules with two of his staff: after Halifax their next port of call was New York. When the ship shuddered he thought she had collided with another vessel, and from experience he expected to be jolted a second time. When he realized they had been torpedoed he ordered his assistants to clear their sections. After collecting his life-jacket from reception he stood by to receive passengers at the main muster station in the lounge. 'We're to stay here,' he told them, 'until all the children have been mustered and placed in the boats.' Passengers were already aware of this ruling.

Several of the passengers in the lounge, library, card-room and bar had already left for their cabins to collect fur coats, rugs and other warm clothing and to retrieve passports and valuables. Others, slower to react, now indicated a similar intention, but Anderson refused to let them go. Instead he directed members of his staff, European and Asian, to find out passengers' requirements and bring requested items up to them. Meanwhile he ensured that all those present were wearing life-jackets.

Among those who had already left the lounge was German refugee Dr Martin Bum. The only treasure he possessed, following the sacking of his home by Nazi storm-troopers, was a collection of antique books and drawings which he meant to preserve if he could. They would have considerable value in America, where he was bound. Although the ship was tilted he saw no sign of panic during his excursion below, and he dutifully returned to the lounge with his burden and waited with many others to be called to the boats.

BBC man Eric Davis, also in the lounge, shared in much general conversation, and he too saw no sign of panic. Everyone seemed to be properly equipped and anxious to obey orders, confident in the well-practised routine. He saw no tears and much thoughtful sharing of coats and rugs. Many cherished hopes that abandonment might not prove necessary.

In the forward end of the lounge, again before Anderson's intervention, sat Lieutenant-Commander Richard Deane, RNVR; he was fifty-six. Deane was on his way to take up a naval appointment in Canada. He had reported to Admiral Mackinnon on embarkation at Liverpool and been considerably piqued at being told his services were not required on the voyage; he had felt it as a slap in the face. Mackinnon even advised him to wear mufti. Surely, on a ship where the disproportion of Asians to Europeans was so great and the cargo so fragile, use could have been made of his expertise and experience. Now, after noting with satisfaction that his fellow passengers were taking things calmly, he slipped down to his cabin to fetch his wife, who had gone to bed early, fully dressed on her husband's advice. Deane had not for one moment believed they were yet out of danger. He helped his wife into a heavy coat, put a coat on himself and buckled his service revolver round his waist; it might come in handy.

After much lobbying, Deane had got himself appointed to take charge of Boat 7, and he took his wife back not to the lounge but to his boat station. Boat 7 was the fourth from the bow on the starboard or weather side, and as the list had developed to port, the angle of the ship was against all the boats on the starboard side, making lowering a ticklish procedure. Several other passengers, apparently ignoring the orders, had assembled on deck instead of in the lounge, and after some trial and error the boat was lowered to the promenade deck.

Two more who escaped to their cabin before Anderson's veto were Letitia Quinton, a forty-one-year-old widow, born and brought up in Canada (where she had met her English naval husband), and her fifteen-year-old son Anthony, hitherto a student at Stowe. 'You're two useless people in England,' Letitia's mother had written from Canada. 'Come over here.' They were in the process of doing so. Tony, who was engrossed in a historical novel about an earlier Continental tyrant – Napoleon – looked up when the lounge vibrated to see a cloud of what he thought was smoke rising from the carpet. Then he realized it was dust. Letitia Quinton, an ample lady of imperious mien, led her son without hesitation down to the cabin, where she stuffed jewellery, passports and money into a capacious and cumbrous handbag before returning with Tony to the lounge.

Tom and Margaret Hodgson, thirty-five and thirty respectively, were playing cards with Alice Bulmer from Wallasey, whose fourteen-year-old daughter Pat had just gone to bed. They were soon joined by Pat and a school friend, Dorothy Galliard, who was travelling to America with the Bulmers. The Hodgsons had sold up in Baildon, Yorkshire for Tom to start a new life with a timber firm in Toronto. All five of them waited for further instructions.

Despite the innumerable drills there was some confusion among passengers as to whether they should stay at their designated muster stations in the lounge, bar or library or make for the boats. There was a natural anxiety not to leave it too long and get left behind, and preference for a move to the boats, as the tilt steepened, became more marked. One who was not content to remain idle any longer was the MP James Baldwin-Webb. 'I think we ought to do something,' he told Letitia Quinton, and he ushered the Quintons out on deck. Their boat station was No. 6, on the lee and listing port side, much the easier. The boat was already loaded, with Lascars in a majority, and Baldwin-Webb took charge. He got the Lascars to help the Quintons and others into the boat, but such was the crush that they were obliged to sit at opposite ends.

Others who were just joining this boat were London publisher Ernest Szekulesz, a Hungarian of morose but tenacious character, and two elderly Dutch refugees, Hirsch and Emma Guggenheim, forced to flee from Holland and now on their way to the Dutch East Indies.

They had sat at the same table as the Quintons and had amazed Tony, no lightweight himself, by their capacity for food. There were none of the evacuee children in this boat, but Florence Croasdaile, the American wife of the British naval officer captured in Norway, was there with Patricia and Lawrence. Even when the boat was almost full and about to be launched, Baldwin-Webb stayed at his post to see the job through. 'I'll join you in a moment,' he told Szekulesz. One of the last to embark in this boat was Admiral Mackinnon.

William Forsyth, director of a travel firm, had been in his cabin pouring a night-cap for the woman he was entertaining – Baroness Emmely von Inglesleben, a German authoress and refugee from the concentration camps – when the cabin disintegrated around them, spilling their drinks and leaving them standing in a profusion of litter and clothing. Neither was hurt, but they could have done with the drinks now. With a rueful glance at the shattered bottles, Forsyth escorted his bemused guest up to the promenade deck. He was greatly encouraged by the behaviour of people around him, especially the women and children.

In the cabin next to Forsyth's, playwright Arthur Wimperis was lying in his bunk reading when there was a terrific crash and the lights went out. Yet, unlike Forsyth's, his cabin suffered little damage. Having written for the theatre since Edwardian days, and more recently for the screen, he had learned to adapt to the times, but the thought that there might be a story here was quickly suppressed. First it was necessary to survive. He donned a raincoat, put his pipe and tobacco in one of the pockets, pulled on his life-jacket, and went up to his boat station, Boat 9 on the starboard side, with Quartermaster Collin in charge. A dozen or more children were already mustered there under Padre King, and more were trailing up from below. Some he judged as still in a state of shock and he did his best to comfort them, but like Forsyth he thought them incredibly brave. Their trust in the crew and in their escorts was unshaken.

Already ensconced in this boat were Nurse Dorothy Smith – the nurse recruited by CORB – and the two boys in quarantine with chickenpox, the five-year-olds Alan Capel and Peter Short. The launching crew had been briefed to embark them on the boat deck, and this was why Derek and Billy had seen nothing of them.

The rallying and mobilization of the other children had continued under Marjorie Day, with Joe Hetherington joining forces whenever his duties allowed. Jollying the children through half-blocked passages, finding detours where necessary, and assisting those who fell or could barely walk, the escorts were relieved to find when they reached the deck that the emergency lighting system had functioned. But in its sepulchral glow they were dismayed to see a pool of blood shining darkly on the deck. The little girl who had been badly hurt was bleeding profusely. Although first aid was expertly applied, her plight had an adverse effect on the younger children, some of whom started to cry.

All the escorts were now at their posts by the boats, however, and the muster of children was almost complete. Apart from the boy known to have been killed, only one child appeared to be missing. Marjorie Day made the rounds of the after boat stations where the children were embarking – Nos. 8, 10 and 12 on the port side and Nos. 9 and 11 on the starboard – and checked each group with their escort. Michael Rennie confirmed that his party was complete. Sybil Gilliat-Smith had her full complement, plus the three Grimmond girls, who had become detached from Mary Cornish's party. Padre King, too, signalled that all was well with his group of boys. Father O'Sullivan and his boys had reached Boat 12, the farthest aft on the starboard side, where Derek Capel and Billy Short were asking about their kid brothers. 'They've been taken care of,' O'Sullivan assured them.

In charge of this boat was Fourth Officer Ronald Cooper, aged twenty-two. Arriving at the boat station straight from his bunk, he found the Lascar crew already mustered. 'Clear away the boat, man the falls, and stand by for lowering,' he told them. But he elected to delay the actual launching, intending to wait for the ship's officers, including the captain, who he knew would be the last to leave.

At Maud Hillman's station the lights had failed and she was asking for a torch. She was hoping to go below to collect blankets, some of her charges – they included the girls from Liverpool and Bess Walder – being flimsily clad. Three factors had conspired to cause this. One, the relaxation of the order to sleep fully clothed; two, the location of the explosion, right under the children's cabins; and three, the darkness, making emergency clothing difficult to find. But Joe Hetherington stopped her. There was no time to delay the embarkation, and they would find blankets in the boats. He helped her get the children in.

Mary Cornish was missing one little girl, and although several crew members had searched the children's quarters and confirmed that they were clear, she felt bound to have one more look. Leaving Rosemary Spencer-Davies in charge of her girls in Boat 10, she hurried below. While she was gone, Boat 10 was lowered to the promenade deck and the children, under orders from the crew, piled in. Seeing that this boat was about to be launched and would be minus an escort, Marjorie Day got in herself and beckoned another escort, Lilian Towns, to follow. Lilian, a New Zealander and herself a mother of two, had been recruited at the last moment as a substitute for a girl deemed unsuitable. There were fifteen children to look after in this boat, including the badly injured girl.

When Mary Cornish eventually returned, anxious and empty-handed, Joe Hetherington directed her into the next boat astern, Boat 12, where Ronnie Cooper, despite pressure from his crew, was determined to hang on as long as possible.

Among Padre King's boys at Boat 9 was the volatile Johnny Baker from Southall. Slippery as an eel, he suddenly started off back to his cabin, calling: 'I've forgotten my life-jacket!' His brother Robert, five years his senior, was the only one quick enough to chase him and catch him. 'Oh no you don't!' The younger boy was much the tougher in build, but size and experience were against him, and despite all his wriggling his brother held on until King came to help. Someone found Johnny a life-jacket, and he struggled no more. It did not occur to him for one moment that it might be his brother's.

Embarking direct from the top deck, where the cabins were situated, were the Choat family, Frank and Sylvia and their three teenage children, Rachel, nineteen, Peter, eighteen, and Russell, sixteen; they were further forward in Boat 4. Frank Choat, Australian born, had been severely wounded at Gallipoli and was physically handicapped; at the convalescent home he had been sent to in Wales he had met Sylvia, whose husband had been killed in the war. They had fallen in love, married and settled in Canada, where they were now returning after a spell in England completing their children's education.

Rachel had just rung the bell to have her bath drawn when the explosion threw her to the floor. Dressed in pyjamas and bedroom slippers, she grabbed a coat and followed the others. The boat deck was a kaleidoscope of running figures and she saw the boat next to theirs going down spasmodically and wondered how it would fare – this was Boat 6. Then she felt her father's hands round her waist as he lifted her firmly into Boat 4. Her mother, bulky with a wad of £5 notes sewn into her jacket, got in next, then the two boys. She didn't realize until later that her invalid father, refusing to enter the boat until others were safely embarked, had been left behind.

In the bar Jimmy Proudfoot, a lanky Glaswegian, judged it was past closing time. He had poured himself a wee dram when the torpedo struck, and now he pocketed a bottle against emergencies, closed the bar, grabbed his life-jacket (reflecting that he'd got his priorities just about right), checked that the children, among whom he had made many friends, were trooping up from below in good order, and made his way to his boat station, astern on the starboard side – Boat 11. Here the third officer, W. J. Lee, had already instructed the Lascar crew on the boat deck to clear away the falls and belly bands for lowering the boat to the promenade deck.

Hearing that one girl was missing and that one of the escorts had gone to look for her, Proudfoot returned to the aft cabins and shouted down the companionway. Eventually, getting no answer, he made his way back via the lounge, where he was surprised to find that many of the passengers assembled by Anderson were still waiting to be called to the boats. It was not his place to interfere – Anderson must know what he was doing – and he rejoined his boat station. On this comprehensive tour he saw no sign of panic on the part of passengers or crew.

Stewardess Annie Ryan had just had a bath and was putting her slacks on when the ship was hit. As she fell to the floor she heard the colleague she shared the cabin with, Margaret Ladyman, scream with surprise as she too was thrown off her feet. Margaret Ladyman had two sons in the RAF and she had been saving up for their birthdays. For all her concern for them, her worst premonitions were for herself. Handing Annie Ryan a package, she asked: 'Will you look after this for me? If anything happens to me, would you see my sons get it?'

The younger woman could not see why she should have any better chance of survival than Margaret, but there was no time to argue. Together they started off along the corridor to collect blankets, which they were sure would be wanted, but a crewman intervened. 'Christ – you can't get them, it's flooded down there.' Making for Boat 10, the two stewardesses were just in time to see heads disappearing below promenade deck level. 'Wait for us!'

Some of the paying passengers nearer the bows slept through the torpedoing and did not awake until they heard the alarm bells. Eleven-year-old Colin Ryder Richardson, travelling alone to join an American family on Long Island by invitation – they had been quite exceptionally solicitous about his welfare, asking for details of his diet, health, character traits and idiosyncrasies, so as to be sure of making him feel at home – was sitting up in bed reading a comic. This fair-haired, round-faced, snub-nosed lad had endeared himself to everyone by his unspoilt, sunny disposition, and one of the Hungarian refugees, a journalist named Laszlo Raskai who occupied the next cabin, had appointed himself as his guardian. Gentle-mannered as Colin was, he would hardly have been conspicuous without the scarlet life-jacket he always wore, specially ordered for him by his mother – who not surprisingly had been no less solicitous than his promised hosts. It was made of waterproof silk lined with kapok, and she had made him promise to wear it at all times. 'You must never take it off until you get to America. Go to bed in it. If you are torpedoed the British Navy will rescue you, even if they take two or three days to come, so don't worry.'

The boy had stubbornly refused to exchange the scarlet jacket for the Board of Trade jacket distributed on board, and after examination, and with due regard to the boy's sensibilities and his promise to his mother, it was passed as equally serviceable. In fact it was better, because it was warmer and, unlike the issue type, had sleeves. 'Young Colin', as the passengers called him at first, became better known as 'Will Scarlet' because of this garment. Now he grabbed his raincoat, dressing-gown and balaclava helmet (specially knitted for him by his mother) and hurried to his boat station, where he expected to join up with his guardian.

As it happened, Laszlo Raskai had not yet gone to bed and he had become involved in the extrication of the evacuee children from crumbling cabins. When he went to collect Colin he found that the boy, sensibly enough, had gone to his boat. Raskai followed and helped Colin into the boat, then stepped back to help others. He helped many more in the next half-hour, but this was the last Colin saw of him.

A rumour that the ship might not sink caused many people to hang back at this stage, and some even climbed back on board. But soon afterwards a final exhortation came from Captain Nicoll.

'Take care of yourselves and get into the boats.'

Joe Hetherington, Second Officer Asher, Third Officer Lee and Fourth Officer Cooper were all at their posts on

the promenade deck, supervising the loading and lowering. Language difficulties with the Asians caused
occasional problems, but embarkation went forward in an
orderly manner and there had been no serious hiccups so
far. No one owned up to rescinding the order for the
children to go to bed fully dressed, which looked like a
serious error, but many were wearing coats over their
pyjamas. Most of the adult passengers were fully clothed
and many wore coats.

Against this the Lascars were all inadequately dressed,
those who had escaped from the engine-room and stoke-
hold wearing nothing more substantial than trousers and
singlets. By Atlantic standards it was not a cold night, but
it was chilly enough, and the experience of being torpedoed on their first Atlantic crossing, 600 or more miles
from land, was no less traumatic for them than for others.
If some passengers gained an impression of swarms of
Asians suddenly descending on their allotted boat
stations, inconveniently cramming the boats, this was
inevitable in a crew where they outnumbered Europeans
by more than four to one.

After helping the ailing Joan Irving to the companionway and up to the promenade deck, Beth Cummings and
Bess Walder got a crew member to carry her to their
boat. This was No. 5, on the starboard side. The list was
becoming more acute and the two girls hung on to each
other to keep their feet. While they were waiting for their
boat to be lowered the auxiliary lighting came on, and
looking round at the faces of the little ones, the five- and
six-year-olds, they thought how brave they were, and how
uncomprehending. The two girls knew enough to realize
the danger they were in, but Patricia Allen, the survivor
of the *Volendam*, reassured them. 'We'll be picked up,
like we were before – you'll see.'

* * *

In the lounge, Dr Martin Bum was clutching his package nervously, getting more and more restive. The black-out curtains were drawn and he couldn't get a glimmer of what was going on outside, but he could hear shouting and he had a powerful presentiment that many others had gone to the boats. Eventually he went out on deck to see for himself, and found the ship fully lit and people scurrying about in breathless but largely controlled animation. Seeing one of the port-side lifeboats being lowered he ran to his own boat which, like Jimmy Proudfoot's, was No. 11 on the starboard side aft.

Noticing Dr Bum disappear, and no less impatient for news, Anderson left the lounge to get instructions. The man he contacted was Second Officer Asher. 'My God!' said Asher. 'Are they still in the lounge? Direct them to the port-side boats first.' These were the boats where the list helped rather than hindered the launching.

Anderson sent the passengers who were still in the lounge on their way and then, measuring the risk and concluding that there was still time, ran to his office, opened the safe, withdrew four sealed packages which had been left with him in safe custody and tied them up in a canvas bag. One package belonged to Arthur Wimperis, another to Eric Davis. Returning to the lounge, he was surprised to find small groups of people still congregated there, passengers who must only recently have arrived. He directed them now to the starboard boats. Soon afterwards Hetherington came into the lounge and Anderson confirmed, on the basis of reports from his staff, that all sections of the passenger accommodation were clear.

Up to this point, as one by one the lifeboats were lowered to the promenade deck for passengers and crew to embark, casualties were few. Two Lascars from the engine-room were unaccounted for, a steward was missing, one child was dead and several more had been injured, but the theory and expectation of a survivable incident still seemed credible. Much would depend, no doubt, on prompt and efficient rescue. But the immediate hazard to be negotiated was the lowering of the boats from the promenade deck, where most were still suspended, to the water – a drop of some forty feet.

For the apprehensive occupants, rocking in mid-air, with an abyss beneath them and little beyond the crush of their bodies to secure them, a process that had been vertiginous even in port and in daylight was translated into something sickeningly precarious in darkness, stormy seas in mid-ocean and a listing ship down by the stern. Each individual launching was supervised by a ship's officer or quartermaster, but on the canting, storm-tossed boat deck it became increasingly difficult for the boat crews to control the falls as boats filled up and the next stage in the lowering began. In boat after boat, on lee and weather side alike, falls became twisted and blocks jammed.

The effect on the equilibrium of the boats was disastrous. As though in some surrealist fairground switchback, they descended in jerky and sporadic asymmetry, their longitudinal balance erratically awry. Clutching the thwarts, the ropes and each other, the unfortunate occupants fought to maintain a handhold, but many of them, dumb with fear or screaming with terror, were pitched headlong into the sea.

There was little the launching crews could do but continue the murderous process; nothing would restore the boats' stability until the falls were unhooked as they became waterborne and their natural buoyancy floated them off. Yet even when afloat their equilibrium remained under threat. As lumpy seas collided with the precipitous hull that beetled above them, great stalagmites of ocean soared into the air, swamping the boats as they fell.

There was another and even more disconcerting contrast between a ship in port or at anchor and a ship in mid-ocean, one that took all but the most seasoned mariners unawares. A torpedoed vessel, as the stricken passengers discovered, does not grind to an immediate halt. Engines may be silenced and stilled, but the effect of past propulsion remains. With braking power totally absent, deceleration is gradual.

As soon as the boats, many of them waterlogged and in danger of capsizing, settled themselves to the rise and fall of the swell, the truth of this maritime principle was mortifyingly revealed. The *Benares*, still under way, was a hazard to her own lifeboats.

4

In the Boats

Arriving at her lifeboat on the starboard side amidships, Beth Cummings was closely followed by Bess Walder. Looking astern they glimpsed the stark outline of the two anti-aircraft guns sited there and thought how useless such weapons were against an enemy who struck in darkness from below. They were brought back to reality by the shouting of the Lascars as they steadied the boat before clambering in. Squeezing in amongst them they joined Joan Irving and another girl who was crying piteously, having been hurt in the torpedoing; she lost consciousness soon after. Meanwhile the launching crew on the boat deck continued lowering the boat into the water.

Suddenly the boat dropped at one end and hung crookedly, forcing the startled occupants to cling like limpets in a frantic endeavour to hold their position. Like a shoal of flying fish a whole group of Lascars plunged or were hurled into the sea. The lifeboat steadied momentarily when it reached the water, but the waves were so powerful that every time they tried to push away from the ship it crashed back against the hull. Several of the displaced Lascars climbed back up the rope ladder to the deck, while the remaining occupants, European and Asian, grabbed the levers of the Fleming gear and worked them vigorously. The liner was sinking lower every minute and they feared it would founder and drag them down with it.

Cadet Doug Critchley, twenty, had been allocated to Boat 1, forward on the starboard side. The two forward boats, port and starboard, were inaccessible from the promenade deck, and their embarkation point was one deck below. Critchley was off watch and in bed when the torpedo struck. Putting on a pair of slippers, a bridge coat and a life-jacket, he hurried down to find that his boat had already been lowered to the water. 'Get into the boat and take the tiller,' ordered Hetherington, and he went down the ladder, cleared the falls and held his position by painter while passengers negotiated the ladder.

Because the ship was still making headway, the two forward boats were caught in a funnel fed by the bow-wave and aggravated by the proximity of the hull. Water slopped over the gunwales of Critchley's boat as the passengers boarded, and although the cadet was a rowing man and accustomed to small boats he could do nothing to stop it. Eventually the boat filled so alarmingly that some of the women turned tail and went back up the ladder.

The first boat on the other side was the chief engineer's boat, and when Macauley reached it several people had managed to get in, although it was still swaying on the blocks. Macauley called for it to be lowered to the water and embarkation continued by rope ladder, but high seas and the funnel effect of the bow-wave quickly flooded it. Something had to be done to lighten it, and Macauley asked a naval signaller to get out to set the example, then ordered four Lascars to follow, which they did, reboarding the ship. This left six Asians and five Europeans, not including Macauley, which the chief engineer thought was about right for this comparatively small boat in its water-logged state. He then climbed back to the deck himself. Seeing a saloon boy carrying buckets, he told him to lower two into the boat, hoping that, by baling, the remaining occupants would be able to reduce the flooding.

John McGlashan, descending from the boat deck, saw what happened to this boat. Struck by a huge sea, it broached to, filled to overflowing with water and drifted away out of control. Buffeted by more heavy seas, it capsized, throwing its occupants into the water. There was nothing McGlashan could do for them, and he moved aft to Boat 4.

As Quartermaster Collin's boat was being lowered it dipped at one end, crash-dived into the swell and threw some of its occupants out. Johnny Baker was at the high end; he held on to the thwart he was sitting on and hung there until he was jerked off. As the boat drifted away, ladders were unfurled from the promenade deck and those in the water were exhorted to climb back up. To a seven-year-old the hull soared like a cliff-face, and he thought he would never get to the top. But at last he made it, to be grabbed by one of the crew. His elder brother had been with him in the boat, but there was no sign of him now.

Another lad in this boat, eight-year-old Jack Keeley, bobbed about on the surface before spotting the ladder and starting to climb it. Ahead of him, moving ponderously, was a sailor with enormous boots who kept treading on the boy's fingers. Soon the sailor became aware of it. 'Let me go on ahead,' he said. 'Put your hand where my boot has just left and you'll be all right.' To the agile Keeley it seemed that the sailor was scarcely moving at all, but he was grateful to him eventually when he lifted him over the rail at the top. 'Why don't you get a blanket?' asked the sailor, appalled at the boy's scanty clothing. All he had on was a kapok waistcoat and life-jacket over pyjama bottoms. But there was no time to go looking for blankets.

Another of the boats, descending jerkily, brought ter-rified screams from the occupants as the after-fall took charge, precipitating the boat into a lop-sided dive into the sea. Marjorie Day saw it happen and was transfixed by it. This boat, she knew, held Sybil Gilliat-Smith's party, and the Grimmond girls as well. The sight of all those bodies and limbs falling in a coagulated mass into the maelstrom below left her limp with horror, but she was a prisoner in her own boat and there was nothing she could do.

Meanwhile her own boat was being lowered, and as this too hovered drunkenly she seized the two children nearest to her and vowed to hold on to them. Somehow the crew on the boat deck re-established control, but on reaching the water the boat pitched and rocked in the backwash from the hull and rapidly flooded. There were thirteen girls in this boat – originally Mary Cornish's party – and Marjorie Day was glad to have the help of two of the stewardesses, Annie Ryan and Margaret Ladyman, as well as Lilian Towns, to help look after them. Rosemary Spencer-Davies, too, was in this boat, and they all knew they could depend on her. But none of them could do anything for the injured girl, who soon lost consciousness, or for her sister, who was suffering from shock. Annie Ryan had brought a first-aid box with her but had lost it when the boat lurched during the launching. These two sisters were the first to die in this boat.

Baldwin-Webb was still collecting stragglers for Boat 6, where Ernest Szekulesz, still preparing himself for the worst, greatly admired the MP's efficient assumption of authority. He heard the man urging another of the continental refugees, Ika Olden, to embark without her husband Rudolf, from whom she had somehow got sep-arated. 'Either he's in one of the other boats,' Baldwin-Webb told her, 'or he'll follow you in a minute.' She turned to a friend she had made on the ship, Professor

J. P. Day, of McGill University; like him she was on her
way to Toronto. 'If you come through, will you take our
love to our little girl?' This was the child who had
preceded the Oldens to Canada. 'We shall *all* come
through,' said the professor. 'Don't worry.' With that she
entered the boat.

Another woman reluctant to enter this boat was sixty-
three-year-old Anne Fleetwood-Hesketh; she had volunteered early in the voyage to help with the children and
had continued to do so. She had already turned down a
place in one boat to give a seat to a child. Eventually
Baldwin-Webb persuaded her to join Szekulesz, the Quintons, the Croasdailes and some thirty Lascars in Boat 6.
He could not delay the launching any longer, however,
and the lowering process began. Again the falls got out of
alignment and the boat struck the water at an angle. Most
of the Europeans held on, but more than half the Lascars
were thrown out.

Tony Quinton was hanging on successfully when he
caught the full weight of a large lady who landed on top
of him, loosening his hold. It was Mrs Fleetwood-
Hesketh. He clung to her grimly, thinking her bulk would
save them both, but they fell out together. Stunned and
bruised, and hampered by obstructions in the water –
oars, ropes, bodies – he splashed about until he found
himself sinking. Strangely relaxed, he resigned himself to
a watery grave. This was it, and he might as well get it
over quickly. He started gulping water, forgetting he was
wearing a perfectly serviceable Board of Trade life-jacket,
which suddenly rocketed him to the surface. There, in his
bemused, punch-drunk state he beheld a scene of *Grand
Guignol* extravagance. All the lights of the ship were
blazing, shedding reflections of enchanting beauty on the
water's corrugated surface. Flotsam from the plunging

lifeboats littered the ocean, heads were bobbing about on the water like lobster-pot floats, and the listing ship, magnificent in its death-throes, was beginning to settle. There was no sign of the lady who had provoked but probably broken his fall.

Through this pandemonium of movement and sound a single voice penetrated. Urgent and peremptory, it brooked no disobedience. He recognized it at once as the voice of his mother. Despite having been precipitated from stem to stern, Letitia Quinton had retained her place in the boat – and her handbag – and now, spotting her son twenty or thirty yards away, she was calling imperiously to him to return. He had never been more appreciative of her clarity of enunciation than in that moment. He roused himself and swam towards the boat, which was now so completely waterlogged that the sea was lapping over the gunwales. Only the prow and the stern were showing. Thus his mother had little difficulty in hauling him in.

Also in this boat was a supernumerary chief engineer on passage to Montreal to join another Ellerman Line ship. He had watched the quartermaster and his Lascar crew lowering the boat and had thought they had the job nicely under control, but when the after end ran away he grabbed a rope and held on, sliding down the rope afterwards to regain the boat. He managed to pull in four people who had been thrown out, after which he held on to the rope to keep the boat near the ship. When no one else appeared he let go and the boat drifted away.

The numbers in this boat had been reduced by a third. One man who was missing, noticed Tony Quinton, was Admiral Mackinnon; he must have got trapped under the boat.

* * *

When the parties from the lounge belatedly reached their embarkation points, all but one of the lee boats was in the water. BBC man Eric Davis, helping at the ladders, noticed one of the sailors trailing a rope to women struggling in the water, casting the line towards them with the skill of an angler. When they grasped it, he dragged them towards the boats like puppets. Admiring this and other examples of crew ingenuity, Davis felt that the passengers, especially the elderly, were remarkably active, performing such daunting feats as descending swaying ladders and ropes. He still saw no sign of panic, although he noted that some of the women had to be persuaded to leave their husbands behind. The only cries of distress came from people struggling in the water.

Here the feats being performed were heroic. One young man who dived repeatedly in an attempt to recover the boys in his charge was the theological student Michael Rennie; he did this so determinedly that his companions in Boat 11 urged him to slow down. 'You'll exhaust yourself,' they warned. 'They've all got life-jackets – we'll pick them up in good time.' But Rennie could see them being tossed hither and thither and feared they would be crushed where they were. 'There's children in the water,' he gasped. 'I've got to get to them.' The others gave what help they could, but few were capable of emulating the athletic Rennie.

Lee kept his boat alongside while the rescue work went on, but meanwhile they were so swamped that they lost oars and sails, washed overboard. At last, with thirty-four people on board, including thirteen children, he cut the painter. At first they tried to bale some of the water out, but they soon gave this up. The boat was awash and the water slopped in faster than they could get rid of it.

Beth Cummings and Bess Walder, in Boat 5, were

struggling with others to get clear by operating the Fleming gear, only to be hurled back repeatedly by the backwash against the ship's side.

Several of the Sunderland girls were in Marjorie Day's boat, and one of them, Eleanor Wright, from the Bede School, saw one of the boys who had somehow escaped the indefatigable rescue work of Rennie – it was Bess Walder's six-year-old brother Louis – come to the surface. Eleanor watched her schoolmate George Crawford lean far out over the side of the boat to drag the gulping child to safety. Eventually he succeeded, but not before he himself had lost his balance and toppled over the side. Caught in one of the rapids between lifeboat and hull, he was swept out of range.

Among the capsized boats, one or two other swimmers were showing themselves almost the equal of Rennie. Outstanding was a thirty-three-year-old Australian named Arthur Dowling, returning home from a business trip to England. Over six feet tall, powerfully built, and prominent in Melbourne as a cricketer and golfer, he too dived again and again to rescue children struggling in the water. Some, unable to help, averted their gaze, haunted by the sight of tiny terror-stricken faces. Finally, Dowling refused to reboard the lifeboat until he had helped push it clear.

Another man who dived in after the children was Colin Ryder Richardson's self-appointed guardian, the Hungarian journalist Laszlo Raskai. But in the mêlée of bodies and boats it was impossible for his colleagues to keep track of his movements, and from one of his rescue attempts he did not return.

Tom and Margaret Hodgson, with Alice and Pat Bulmer and Pat's schoolfriend Dorothy, were among those late in leaving the lounge. When they finally reached their boat station the ship was well down in the water and the deck was almost awash. Helped over the rail by her husband, Margaret Hodgson thought she would be stepping straight into a boat, but it had already been launched and was some distance away. The others followed her and they swam towards it, but no sooner had they reached it than it overturned.

Margaret and Pat, both strong swimmers, reached another boat and were hauled in, recognizing the Digby-Mortons as their rescuers. But neither Margaret's husband Tom, nor Pat's mother Alice, nor her schoolfriend Dorothy, reappeared after the capsizing.

In charge of this boat was a twenty-five-year-old seaman from the Isle of Lewis named Angus Macdonald; trained as a carpenter, he so loved the sea that he volunteered for the merchant navy when the war started, although in a reserved occupation. Colin Ryder Richardson was in this boat, comparatively snug in his waterproofed silk life-jacket. The ship was still close enough for him to hear the water roaring into her hull. Also dragged into this boat after sliding down a rope and plunging into the swell was the sixty-year-old Canadian Professor Day.

Lieutenant-Commander Richard Deane, at Boat 7 on the weather side, assembled his complement on the promenade deck and helped a number of women to board, among them his wife, then got in himself. To assist him he had another serviceman, the French lieutenant Hervé de Kerillis, and a quartermaster. As they were lowered to the water the Schat skids eased the inevitable friction against the hull on this convex side, and they reached the water without any of the jamming that had afflicted so many other boats. Then their difficulties began.

Denied the more active role he had sought until now,

Deane was frustrated to find that the hand-propelled Fleming gear had not been properly fitted – or if it had it had been damaged in the launching. Instead of being able to propel themselves swiftly clear of the hull, they were helpless. All they could find was a single oar, and even this splintered as Deane battled with it to fend the boat off.

Although this was the weather side and there was a heavy swell, there was no great breaking sea, to Deane's relief. His aim now was to get away aft, but he soon saw that the boats astern of him would be in the way, so he changed his mind and tried to push the boat forward. With the ship still moving in that direction progress was painfully slow, and meanwhile the backwash of the swell kept crashing against them and slopping freely over the gunwales. Seeing this, Deane shouted up to the promenade deck: 'Someone throw me a bucket!'

Someone did – it was Joe Hetherington – and Deane and his crew began baling.

Although all the boats except one had been launched, with varying fortunes, there were still several people stranded on board. Among them was an energetic little brunette named Doris Walker from Tenterfield, New South Wales, a children's nurse whose employment in England had ended and who had been unable to get a berth back to Australia until now. With her two cabin companions she had descended a rope ladder only to see her lifeboat capsize in front of her. The horror of seeing drowning children at such hideously short range had paralysed her temporarily, but she could do nothing to help them and after much exhortation from Joe Hetherington and others, and despite the lurching of the ship, she returned with her companions to the deck. Directed to another boat, she made a second uncertain descent, only for the lifeboat to drift tantalizingly out of reach. Once again she climbed back to the promenade deck. But now she had lost touch with her companions.

Presiding over what had become a bewildering succession of traumas and tragedies was the giant chief officer, still somehow preserving an exterior of calm. But around him his world was disintegrating. Luminous distress flares – amber, white and red – striated the sky, the phosphorescence of life-jackets stippled the water, and a brief but brilliant glow from the U-boat's searchlight combined with angry, scudding clouds and an intermittent moon to paint a battle scene of unbearable beauty. Five elderly ladies who had confusedly collected in the dining-room and who had been discovered and directed to the deck by John McGlashan gazed in dumb astonishment at the kaleidoscope of chaos and colour before them. 'Look!' said one. 'There's the boat that's come to rescue us!' But McGlashan, following the pointing finger, knew better. 'That's the U-boat that torpedoed us.'

With the enemy so near, fears that another torpedo might be fired to finish them off hastened their movements. But when it came to descending a ladder the ladies not surprisingly balked. The only hope, thought McGlashan, was to get them away on a raft.

Whether for reasons of economy or humanity or both, Bleichrodt had no thought of hastening the demise of the *Benares*. Her wounds were clearly mortal; she would go down soon enough. And he was saving his torpedoes for the other ships in the scattered convoy. The freighter *Marina*, hit soon after the *Benares*, had already sunk.

Alex Macauley took a last look at the engine-room and saw that the sea now engulfed the engines. Going forward along the boat deck for a final word with Captain Nicoll, he found him standing alongside No. 3 Hatch with his life-jacket on as though ready to leave. Macauley told him his own boat had become waterlogged and what he had done to rectify the situation.

'You can't do any more,' said Nicoll. 'You'd better look out for yourself.'

'What about you, Captain Nicoll?'

Nicoll waved him away. 'Save yourself, Mac.'

Hetherington, too, was making a final round of the ship. Looking in at the radio cabin on the boat deck, he found the operators, Alistair Fairweather and John Lazarus, the Canadian, still at their posts. Their distress message, giving a position of 56.43 North, 21.15 West, had been acknowledged by the shore station at Lyness in Scotland at 22.06, but there was no news yet of a rescue vessel. Meanwhile they were maintaining radio contact.

Fairweather, calm and collected and smoking a cigarette, gave Hetherington a look that told him he had resolved to stay till the end. Lazarus, too, was making no move.

Hetherington checked the engineers' quarters and found them vacant, then made a final tour of the public rooms. Finally he opened the engine-room door, as Macauley had done, and saw that the flooding was increasing each minute. The ship was listing heavily now and sinking by the stern – it could not be long before she took her final plunge.

Lastly he reported to Captain Nicoll. 'I don't think there's anything more to be done. There's a raft on the lee side – we can make that all right.'

'I think the high side is safer,' said Nicoll. But he showed no inclination to go.

Like any seaman in wartime, Nicoll had known that this moment might come. He had no desire for a watery grave, and the life-jacket he was wearing suggested he would take his chance when the ship sank. But Hetherington, meeting his captain's gaze, half-sensed the resolve that lay behind the poker face. You never knew quite what Nicoll was thinking; but Hetherington thought he knew now. After shaking hands they went their separate ways, Hetherington down to the stern, Nicoll back to the bridge.

Anderson, too, made a final report to his captain. 'All cabins and public rooms are clear. There's still a few passengers on board but we'll get them away on rafts.' Nicoll thanked him, and then, getting no other reaction, Anderson added: 'We'd better leave soon.'

Nicoll said simply: 'It's my duty to stay.'

In most circumstances Anderson might have urged on Nicoll the advantages to himself, to his family and above all to the war effort of personal survival. But both men had seen groups of children, many of them of kindergarten age, shot into the sea like so much refuse. They knew that already there had been tragic losses, and that exposure and hypothermia must take further toll before rescue could come. It was not a scenario that any captain of Nicoll's time could contemplate surviving, and after a handshake he wished Anderson good luck before turning back to the bridge. There, just in case he should survive inadvertently – or so Anderson construed – he locked himself in.

Returning from her search for the missing child, and directed into Boat 12 by the chief officer, Mary Cornish had joined Father O'Sullivan and the six boys he had shepherded together. There was only one paying passenger in this boat, and this was Polish shipping manager Bohdan Nagorski, of the Gdynia-Amerika Line; he had been driven out of Danzig by the Nazis. The experience had not noticeably marred his exterior of well-groomed, even opulent, gentility. Immaculate now in black overcoat, Homburg hat and kid gloves, his attire contrasted starkly with the lightly clad Lascars, of whom eighteen were already in this boat.

Cooper knew he should have more than six children, and although the assistant steward, George Purvis, reported that all the children had cleared their muster stations, Cooper sent him to make a final search. Purvis confirmed on his return that many of the cabins had been wrecked and that the water down there was up to his waist. Like Proudfoot before him he had shouted down the passageway but received no reply. Nevertheless Cooper still held on, resisting the natural anxiety of those around him to get going. He knew that Hetherington and Anderson were still somewhere on board, and then there was Captain Nicoll. Not until he realized that the captain had no intention of saving himself did he give the order to lower away. He still hoped to see the chief officer and the purser.

With the way on the ship now virtually spent, the boat was launched smoothly and remained stable once in the water, escaping the flooding that had befallen all other boats but Boat 4. Cooper then ordered the four Lascars who had been standing by the falls, as well as Purvis, to descend by the side ladders into the boat. After seeing Hetherington and Asher freeing rafts, he made his way into the lifeboat himself.

The handles of the Fleming gear were shipped and there were plenty of willing hands to push-pull away from the vessel. The boys even started a chorus of 'Roll out the Barrel'. Just as they were getting clear, four Lascars – the men who had been operating the falls from the boat deck – scrambled down lifelines and shouted after them in some agitation. They thought they were being abandoned. Cooper had forgotten they were not already aboard and he immediately put back for them. Hetherington, who had also been shouting to Cooper to return, calmed the Lascars and watched them safely away. As Cooper had guessed, he was planning to escape himself on a raft.

Meanwhile salvoes of spindrift and sleet, chilling pyjama-clad bodies, soon silenced the singing.

Unknown as yet to Hetherington, an entire family was still searching for some avenue of escape: these were the Bechs, Marguerite and her three children, Barbara, Sonia and Derek. They had all been in bed at the time of the torpedoing, Derek and his mother in one cabin, the two girls in another. The pungent odour of high-explosive poured into the corridor and seeped into their cabins, but after donning their life-jackets – Sonia did not forget her camel-hair coat – they groped along the corridor and climbed the stairs to their muster station in the lounge. There, appreciating that the sponsored children were to be embarked first, they waited.

Like many others, they found, when they finally went to their boat station on Anderson's direction, that they had tarried too long. Their boat – Boat 4 – was missing, having already been launched. But the task had been completed in an orderly manner, there had been no jamming of falls, and the boat was just pulling away seawards. On board were ten female and two male passengers, twenty-one Lascars, and two crewmen. Barbara, as the eldest of the children, was the first to shin down the rope, setting the example to the others, and Derek, the youngest, followed, his school cap and blazer adding an incongruous but colourful touch. Barbara made it, stepping into the boat just in time, but Derek was seconds too late. He was halfway down the ladder when the boat, caught in a violent backwash, was swept out of reach. It was too far for the most athletic leap, the waters were swollen and turbulent, and he was not a strong enough swimmer to overcome the powerful currents that swirled and eddied at his feet. Meanwhile Barbara, although reaching the lifeboat, collapsed with the effort. She did not see what happened to Derek and feared he must have been lost. In fact, he remounted the swaying ladder, to be grabbed by a watchful seaman at the top. There he rejoined his mother and Sonia.

'Go forward – go up the deck!'

Marguerite Bech followed this instruction reluctantly, not knowing whether Barbara had made it or not. Yet she was galvanized by the urgency to do all she could to save Sonia and Derek. With the stern sinking deeper, however, it was impossible to get forward, and the bows were lifting too high in the air to encourage a jump. Then another voice tugged her in the opposite direction.

'Come quickly – we'll find rafts!' It was Eric Davis, and they followed him uncertainly to the stern.

After saying good-bye to his skipper, Alex Macauley went down to the promenade deck, looked over the starboard side, and saw that all boats on that side had been launched. One of them, however, Boat 3, was not far away. After sliding down a lifeline into the water he swam to this boat and was pulled in by a passenger. No sooner was he aboard than irresistible currents carried the boat under the forefoot of the liner, half-capsizing it and throwing everyone at the aft end into the sea. Those in the bow, Macauley among them, were trapped under water, jammed between lifeboat and hull.

Suddenly the boat righted itself and shot forward, springing the trap. Macauley managed to pull five people

– Second Officer Asher, the chief yeoman of signals, the
fifth engineer, and two Jewish male refugees – back into
the boat, to add to the four Lascars who had been trapped
with him under water. This, thought Macauley, should be
an easily manageable load. But the Fleming gear was
damaged, the rudder was destroyed, the mast was gone
and they were swamped. Meanwhile, as the bows of the
Benares soared more and more steeply above them, they
knew the sinking was imminent.

Boat 1, with Cadet Critchley in charge, also drifted or
was drawn under the liner's bows; but by propelling
themselves vigorously they managed to avoid the fate of
Macauley's boat. They reached what they felt was comparative safety, about fifty yards from the ship.

One of the two boys who had climbed back on board,
Johnny Baker, eventually regained his original boat,
Quartermaster Collin somehow persuading it back to the
ship's side. There Johnny found himself reunited with
Padre King's boys, also Alan Capel and Peter Short, with
Dorothy Smith as nurse/escort. He got a special welcome
from Arthur Wimperis and William Forsyth, both great
admirers of the evacuee children.

If some of the Lascars had seemed to crowd the boats
early on, others, mostly members of the launching crews
on the boat deck, were among the last to embark. Richard
Deane in Boat 7 was still pushing forward when four
Lascars slid down the ropes into his boat. Short of able-
bodied men as he was, he was glad to have them. But he
wondered how many more might alight in his boat in this
way. Deciding there was no room for more, and fearing a
crush, he was ruthless enough to finger his revolver,
preparing to use it if his boat should be rushed.

Jack Keeley, the second boy who had climbed back on
the ship, saw rafts being thrown off the stern and felt that

here was his chance. As he hurried aft the ship tilted so much that he overbalanced; one moment he was running along the deck, the next he was in the water. Whether he had been thrown off or washed off he didn't know. What was certain was that he was being dragged down by some inexorable force, some suction so powerful that it even dragged off his boots. They were new ones, too, bought for the journey, and in his abstraction he felt their loss as a tragedy. He would never be able to find those boots. He still seemed to be going down when the descent suddenly ceased and he plopped to the surface. Not far away was one of the rafts he had seen being launched, with a man sitting on it. He shouted and began splashing towards it, but the gap only widened.

Among those releasing rafts at the stern, in addition to the chief officer, were Eric Davis and John McGlashan. The second engineer could feel the ship going down under his feet, which were already awash. Waving to the bridge to try and attract Captain Nicoll's attention, and getting no answering signal, he walked into the sea and swam to a raft. Somehow in those final stages he had split his head open, he didn't know how, and blood was pouring down his forehead, restricting his vision. Alone on the raft, he wound a handkerchief round his skull. He was the man sitting on the raft that Jack Keeley was trying to reach.

Nineteen-year-old Tommy Milligan, the seventh engineer, had taken charge of the launching of another raft, and Davis watched him trying to hold it in position for a woman – it was the Australian nurse Doris Walker – to climb down a rope ladder. A gust of wind caught the ladder, the swell nearly overturned the raft, and the girl fell into the water. Somehow Milligan drew the raft back towards her with an adroit turn of the wrist, and she swam strongly to it and clambered on.

The Bech family appeared at this point and Milligan called out to them: 'Go down the rope. There's a raft at the bottom.' Releasing the two children, whom she had held on to with grim foreboding since missing the lifeboat, Marguerite surrendered them to Milligan's care. She couldn't see what happened to them but soon Milligan was signalling to her to jump overboard after them. They were on the same raft as Doris Walker. By what seemed to Marguerite a miracle, she jumped and landed beside them on the raft. Her worries now switched to Barbara.

Eric Davis and Tommy Milligan also reached this raft, but it was dangerously overloaded and in imminent danger of being sucked down with the ship. Slipping back into the water, Davis set about towing it clear.

On his way down from the bridge, Anderson ran into the ship's baker, Archie McAlister; he was looking for a missing saloon steward. 'He must have gone to the boats,' yelled Anderson. 'Come on, hurry up or we've had it.' Both men judged it too late to go to the stern, and without stopping for further consultation they separated, McAlister jumping over the port side and Anderson the starboard. Floating on his back in his life-jacket, Anderson found himself directly under the bows, which were now almost perpendicular. As the ship went down it would take him with it. Although a non-swimmer he could manage a dog-paddle, and he could see only one chance. Working his way in towards the prow until he could touch it, he thrust his feet against it and kicked with all his strength. This gave him just the impetus he needed, and by primitive arm movements he somehow extended the plunge.

McAlister, on the port side, was luckier. In the first place he could swim, and in the second he was within striking distance of one of the unflooded boats, Boat 4, where he was quickly pulled in. He joined another crewman, ship's carpenter Ewan McVicar, and they shared command of the boat.

Looking up from the adjacent boat, Ernest Szekulesz saw Baldwin-Webb standing alone at the rail preparing to jump, just as McAlister had done; he had done all he could on the deck. But the MP was an older and bulkier man, and it seemed to Szekulesz that he misjudged his distance. His body hit the water like the flat of an oar and showed no animation. He was carried under, and Szekulesz did not see him again.

Water was now flooding over the stern and Hetherington, after launching another raft, was pitched over the side as the ship's bows reached the vertical. As he boarded the last of the rafts he glimpsed the silhouette of the U-boat, now heading purposefully westward to chase its new quarry.

Eric Davis, having pulled the crowded raft clear, looked round for another. Like the boy Keeley he saw a raft with a lone figure on it, and he made that his target.

The Bech children, now clear of the suction, looked back in awe at the uptilted liner. It was still shedding a mosaic of shadow and light, and Sonia, surveying her camel-hair coat, was sickened to find it sleek and shiny with oil. Yet awe and dismay were both foreign to these two youthful and ebullient spirits. With the ship in its death-throes they shared an irreverent regret: 'What a waste of good ice cream!'

The *City of Benares* was about to perform a valedictory all-star spectacular. Through some electrical freak, every light in the ship blazed forth with dazzling brilliance and she glowed like a Chinese lantern, creating the illusion of a consuming internal conflagration. When the sea reached her generators there was a single muffled explosion and then, as though unwillingly, in reluctant slow motion, she subsided stern first, leaving a blinding, briefly impenetrable darkness. The last gleam of light to be snuffed out was the glow from her bridge.

Heinrich Bleichrodt, looking back at the scene from the fast-disappearing *U48* – he was chasing a tanker – noted in his log that the liner had sunk in thirty-one minutes.

5

A Night of Horror

Fears that suction as the ship went down would drag lifeboats and rafts to the depths proved illusory. Instead, the displacement of ocean caused by the *Benares'* 11,000 tons precipitated a tidal bore which threatened some of the boats with capsizing.

Boat 1, with Doug Critchley in charge, had already been flooded by the rapids and mill-races that swirled round the bows of the ship. Propelling themselves by the hand-levers, the twenty-odd people who had boarded this much smaller boat managed to put some fifty yards between themselves and the vortex of the sinking. They were trying to pull two more people into the boat when they were caught broadside-on by the tidal wave. Water-logged and overloaded as the boat was, it capsized. There were no children in this boat – they had all been embarked amidships or astern – and the adult occupants, some of them crewmen, tried to right it by means of a rope that encircled the keel, fitted specially for this purpose; but they tugged and heaved in vain.

As vision acclimatized to the sudden extinguishing of light, those in the starboard boats had their first sight of the port boats, and vice versa. Hitherto they had been masked by the ship. So many boats were flooded to the gunwales, with only stem and stern showing, that the occupants shared a bizarre illusion: they looked like groups of people sitting unsupported in the sea.

The man who noted this simile, and slotted it away for

possible future reference, was playwright Arthur Wimperis, who was himself wallowing in a flooded boat full of children. But at least he was one of the seated, however moistly and uncomfortably. Those spilled out of capsized boats had no time for such picturesque thoughts.

Exhorting his companions to hang on to the keel, Critchley swam off to retrieve an elderly woman, and she hung on for a time. But she soon lost her grip on the greasy metal keel. Twice more Critchley went after her and brought her back when she lost her grip, but eventually she flung out her arms in despair and drifted away.

Most of the others clinging to the boat seemed to have a reasonably sure grip, but within half an hour their numbers had thinned out dramatically. When Critchley spotted a small raft he abandoned his hold on the boat and swam for it, accompanied by naval signaller Mayhew. Three Asians aboard the tiny raft feared they might be dislodged and there was a fight for possession before Mayhew punched his way on and dragged Critchley after him. Seeing this, Mayhew's colleague Micky Goy stayed where he was on the keel of the lifeboat.

Another boat completely inundated by the tidal bore held Beth Cummings and Bess Walder, together with twelve other evacuee children. When the deluge had passed they found themselves up to their necks in water, only the buoyancy tanks inside the boat keeping it afloat, albeit in a submerged state. They perched themselves astride the gunwale, one leg trailing inside the boat and one outside, as though riding a bicycle, while holding on to each other for support. Most of the children and some of the Lascars had gone.

For a time the boat remained stable, but in heavy seas it tossed from side to side, shedding anyone whose hold was inferior. In the end it did what it continually threatened to do – it turned turtle and flung everyone off.

Beth felt herself sinking to what seemed unfathomable depths, down and down until she was sure she was drowning. Something or someone was falling with her and she grabbed at it gratefully, but it was nothing more than a piece of driftwood, too insubstantial to support her. Yet it helped her rise to the surface. She was really frightened now, fighting for breath and realizing for the first time that she might not survive. It was some little time before she spotted the overturned lifeboat some distance away, with several figures hanging on to it. Although she was a non-swimmer and the waves towered above her, she waited for a trough, took a deep breath, decided her direction and flailed her arms at the wave-crests. Some unsuspected current seemed to assist her, and to her astonishment she dead-heated with Bess, who was just climbing on to the keel when she got there.

There were ten or a dozen people, Europeans and Asians, already clutching the keel for support, five or six on each side. In a brief shaft of moonlight Beth saw a hand next to hers suddenly sparkle: the hand belonged to someone on the other side of the boat whom she could not see, but it was distinctive enough, being adorned by a magnificent solitaire diamond ring, the like of which she had never seen before. One of the refugees, she thought – that would be it.

As the minutes passed, wind and sea increased in violence and they were continually drenched in spindrift and foam. But surely someone would come along to pick them up soon. They had perfect confidence that this would happen. Yet there seemed to be no indication that any vessel had stopped. Puzzled, but far from despairing, they simply hung on. Preoccupied with their own problems, they did not notice at first how the prostrate figures opposite and beside them were thinning out. Next time Beth thought to look, the hand with the solitaire ring had gone.

Soon afterwards Beth too lost her grip on the keel and slid down the convex surface into the water. Grabbing the rope that encircled the underside, she found that this gave her a much better purchase. The keel was too oily and slippery for permanent adhesion, and both girls shifted their grip to the rope. They would have preferred to lie parallel to the keel, to keep their legs out of the water, but the curve of the boat was too steep. They had to lie at right angles to it, which meant that not only their legs but also the lower part of their bodies were immersed for most of the time. They lay on the same side of the keel facing each other, with the rope in between.

Bess had retained her glasses so far, but they were continually slipping. She couldn't let go of the rope, so every time she felt them loosening she nudged them back against her shoulders. If she lost her glasses she was lost altogether – she had to be able to see.

They had not settled long when a raft went by holding three people they knew. One of them was the escort Maud Hillman, the others were the two flaxen-haired Liverpool children Joan and James Spencer. They could hardly imagine a more joyless, pitiful sight. Forsaken and derelict, they could have little chance of survival. Already Maud Hillman was struggling to keep the two children secure.

Where were the rescue ships? If they didn't come soon it would be too late. They began to doubt whether help was really at hand. These two buxom teenagers, one from the north and one from the south, while refusing to despair, were reluctantly accepting that they might have to hang on till daylight. They'd be picked up all right then, though, that was for sure.

Their spirits rose sharply as a lifeboat hove into view and they shouted to be taken aboard. But this was one of the waterlogged boats, its equipment ejected on launching, its crew forced to drift out of control. They had no means of diverting to help the four figures – two girls and two Lascars – who were still clinging to life on the upturned boat.

Those who had found and retained a place in the boats were the envy of those who had not. Yet their prospects were scarcely superior. Numbed by perpetual immersion up to their waists and sometimes their chests, lambasted by blinding sleet and a whiplash wind, they too peered in vain for some sign of rescue.

The SOS transmitted by Fairweather and Lazarus was acted on by the Commander-in-Chief Western Approaches twenty-three minutes after it was received at Lyness. The nearest warships available were those escorting the next westbound convoy, OB 214, which was 300 miles astern of the *Benares*. The destroyer *Winchelsea* had left OB 213 twenty-two hours earlier, and although it might be marginally nearer it was escorting an incoming convoy, which was inevitably accorded priority. The senior escorting vessel for OB 214 – the destroyer HMS *Hurricane*, under Lieutenant-Commander Hugh Crofton Simms, RN – was the craft chosen to assist the *Benares*. The signal received by Simms read: 'Proceed with utmost despatch to position 56.43 21.15, where survivors are reported in boats.'

Lieutenant Peter Collinson, ship's surgeon and cipher

officer, took the decoded message to Simms at ten minutes past midnight, just over two hours after acknowledgement by Lyness of the distress message. 'Utmost despatch?' queried Simms. 'We'll do our best.' But he was many hours' steaming from the position given, and because of the heavy seas that were running he could not increase to maximum speed or anywhere near it without risking damage to his ship. At present he was limited to about 15 knots, and even if conditions improved he couldn't hope to reach the survivors until after midday.

Tony Quinton tried, as an exercise, to count the other boats in sight; it took his mind off his plight and gave him something to do. Sometimes he thought he could see several at once but some proved ephemeral, gone before he could count, masked by the peaks of the breakers. Then, when his own boat sank into a trough, he could see no boats at all. Even from the top of the crests he couldn't be sure he wasn't counting the same lifeboats twice. Eventually, although accepting that the margin for error was wide, he believed that over a period he saw ten different boats.

As a further exercise in mind occupation, the ex-Stowe schoolboy, sitting now near his mother in the stern, studied his companions with interest. He counted twenty-two in all. Sitting in the bows and seeming, from his aloof, self-sufficient manner, to distance himself from the whole nightmare proceedings was a man of indeterminate age with a strong Yorkshire accent whose name Quinton didn't know, but taking account of his tweed suit and cap, his no-nonsense, down-to-earth air and the empty pipe clamped in his mouth that he pulled on ruminatively, Quinton thought him astonishingly reminiscent of J. B.

Priestley and dubbed him as such. The man beheld and occasionally commented, but did not seem to partake.

Nearer the middle of the boat were the Hungarian publisher Ernest Szekulesz, whose inveterate pessimism, as Quinton soon recognized, was a kind of carapace protecting him from anticipated disappointments; the American woman Florence Croasdaile and her two children; two of the evacuee boys who had been thrown out of other boats; Monika Lanyi, the daughter of Thomas Mann, grieving for her husband whom she feared had drowned; and the elderly Dutch Jews Hirsch and Emma Guggenheim. The only crew members were ten Lascars, plus the supernumerary chief engineer. Of the Lascars Quinton noted two in particular: one, an NCO of some kind, tall and vigorous and unfailingly cooperative, he called Gunga Din; the other, whose peculiar white headgear, aquiline features and solemn, lugubrious mien lent him an aristocratic sneer in the half-light, he dubbed Basil Rathbone.

Letitia Quinton, seeing that her son was in good order, asked nothing more. A model of good sense and stoicism, she was deferred to by the two men who did most to keep this boat stable, the supernumerary engineer and the Lascar whom Quinton had nicknamed Gunga Din.

'Lifeboat ahoy! We are swamping! Will you please come over!'

Second Officer Hugh Asher had been one of the last to leave the ship. Eventually, with four others, he had managed to reach Alex Macauley's boat, but although the buoyancy tanks prevented it from actually sinking it was completely submerged. For almost an hour Asher wearied himself hailing other boats to take them off, but although his cries were heard few were in any position to help.

Eventually Asher, the engineer and Bartlett transferred to Marjorie Day's boat, where they were little better off, leaving Macauley in the submerged boat with two male Jewish passengers and four Lascars. One of the Lascars was the deck serang, and he stood up in the boat flashing a torch at intervals, trying to maintain contact with other boats.

Macauley had bruised himself badly when he was trapped between lifeboat and hull, and he was glad of the deck serang's help. He closed his mind to everything except the need to keep contact. Then when rescue came they would not be left out.

Marjorie Day's boat, although a lee-side boat, had not escaped flooding either, and tragedy had struck early with the death of the two sisters. But thirteen children still remained. This boat, like many others, had lost all its equipment in the launching, and improvised balers – a hat brought on board by Lilian Towns and a number of shoes – made little impression. The senior escort hoped Asher would prove an acquisition, but he was too exhausted to do much. So far as improving their conditions was concerned they were helpless; all they could do was protect the children as far as they could and keep a look-out for the rescue ship that, like everyone else, they expected to see.

For the first few hours the children responded to the encouragement of their escorts and retained their animation. But then, as the seas broke relentlessly over them and the air temperature fell, they became more subdued. The eldest of the Sunderland girls, Eleanor Wright, joined with Rosemary Spencer-Davies in trying to revive their spirits, as did the escorts and the two stewardesses, Annie Ryan and Margaret Ladyman, but soon they lapsed into a worrying quiescence. 'We mustn't let them fall asleep,' counselled Marjorie Day, fearing the onset of hypothermia, and they slapped the children's faces and massaged their limbs, holding them above water in turn. But all too rapidly they became comatose; their lives were ebbing away.

Where were the ships? Why hadn't they come before now? The lights they occasionally saw, and the torches that flashed intermittently, came only too obviously from other lifeboats. If rescue came now it might still be in time for some, but only a miracle could save these little mites.

When a raft drifted by and the escorts learnt that the survivors had brandy aboard they claimed it for the children and urged them to sip. Whether this retarded or accelerated their regression no one could say, but soon afterwards the younger ones just fell asleep. They did not seem to suffer, nor did they show any symptoms of fear or apprehension. Trustful to the last, they simply fell into a coma from which nothing could rouse them.

All but the two older girls, Rosemary and Eleanor, perished in succession in the space of a few minutes in exactly this way.

Another casualty was the stewardess who had had the premonition, Margaret Ladyman. Before she died she reminded Annie Ryan of her promise to contact her two RAF sons. Reassured that this would be done, she expired almost contentedly. Not so three of the Lascars. Exposed to conditions totally foreign to them, which few of the older ones could hope to survive for long, they suffered untold agonies before extinction mercifully came.

The thirty-eight people in Angus Macdonald's boat – the boat that held the engaging lad Colin Ryder Richardson – were in similar plight. Although he was sitting more than waist-deep in water, and sometimes having to stand,

Colin's cheerful pipe of a voice carried above the howl of the elements to all those around him. Although a boy who had always been close to his mother, he had not been mollycoddled and was no namby-pamby; indeed she had encouraged him to live as much of an outdoor life as possible after the invitation came for him to go to New York. To his companions in the boat he seemed to have physical and mental resources which his immaturity of body and mind scarcely accounted for. Even in those few days on the ship the Canadian Professor Day, who was sitting near him in the boat, had marked him out as an unusually level-headed and sensitive child.

As lumps of ocean smashed into their faces and ran down their chests and backs, they kept the boat from capsizing by throwing what weight they could muster first to port and then to starboard on 'Chippie' Macdonald's shouted instructions. Colin, despite his lack of inches, invariably contributed more than his weight to the balance.

Also in this boat were Margaret Hodgson (who had lost touch with her husband Tom when they swam from the ship), fourteen-year-old Pat Bulmer (who had similarly become separated from her mother and feared she had drowned), and the Digby-Mortons, Henry and Phyllis. The others were mostly women and Lascars, and they suffered almost equally from the cold.

The extent of their immersion varied with their position in the boat and with individual size. For Colin, near the stern, the water sometimes came up to his chest, while Pat Bulmer, amidships, had to stand on a locker at one point to keep head and shoulders uncovered. Although the water protected them from the wind, the warmth of their bodies was draining away. Even this, though, had its compensations as the temperature of the water in the boat perceptibly rose. The most sensuous personal pleasure, for all its evanescence, was the warmth of their own urine coursing around their loins. Then yet another breaker would flood through the boat and the chill would strike worse than before.

Phyllis Digby-Morton sat for hour after hour clasping the broken-hearted Pat Bulmer to her bosom, trying to console her for the loss of her mother, and it seemed of her schoolfriend, and assuring her that rescue would come. 'On your honour, do you believe it?' The girl was never wholly satisfied with the answer.

It was a question that Colin did not need to ask. His mother had promised him that if his ship were torpedoed and sunk the Navy would rescue him, and he believed her. Even in his pyjamas he was warmer than most in his silk-faced life-jacket, and when he felt in the pocket of his raincoat he found a pair of string gloves, the ideal texture for gripping the gunwale. No wonder he trusted his mother.

Colin's male companions tried to shield him from the incessant barrage of water, but some were in worse state than he. Pelted by hailstorms and rain, they faced fierce downpours that lashed them implacably. For the cadaverous build of the Asians the cold and the wind-chill proved fatal, and one by one in startling succession they dropped from their places. One minute they were chattering and praying, the next they were dribbling and incoherent, until finally they fell forward into the water, often in attitudes of prayer, after which nothing but bubbles came up.

After witnessing all this, Colin suffered the macabre experience of being bumped and bruised by the bodies of dead Lascars as they jostled against each other inside the boat. Something had to be done to dispose of them, and there was no one left but Colin to help Macdonald do it. The professor, sixty years old, was too weak to lend a hand, but Colin performed the grisly task with no sign of fear or distaste, yet with proper respect for the dead.

Only when the bodies floated back in again and nearly knocked him out of the boat did the boy briefly recoil. But after a shudder he played a full part in returning them whence they came.

One of the ship's nurses recruited by Anderson was in this boat, and she did all she could for the Asians, but the scenes she was witnessing so filled her with horror that at length her mind was affected. 'Lift up my head!' she called shrilly. 'I'm going – I'm going!' Macdonald, who had put out a sea anchor, was fully absorbed in preventing the boat from capsizing, and the professor already had a woman's head in his lap and was trying to keep her nose and mouth out of the water, so it was Colin who held out his arms to the nurse. In her confused state she kept twisting and turning, and Colin was too small to support her completely. All he could do was let her body and legs float out beside him and keep her head clear of the surface. 'There'll be a boat coming soon,' he told her. 'It won't be long now.' The professor heard his high-pitched voice many times as he tried everything he could think of to bolster the young woman's morale. 'I think I see a light,' he said, falling back on his imagination. 'It could be a ship.' These and other figments he used again and again. He stroked the girl's hair and held her hand, quietening her for a time, but at length she resumed her contortions. 'Goodbye, goodbye,' she called. 'I'm dying, I'm dying.' Still he soothed her with talk, massaged her head and her hands and promised her repeatedly that a ship would soon come.

Once, in a rare lucid moment, she asked poignantly:

'Are the children all right?' When, towards morning, she stiffened and responded no more, Macdonald said gently: 'Colin, she's dead. She's been dead for some time. You must push her overboard.'

'I can't do it.'

'You did it to the others, Colin. You've done all you can for her. It can't be helped. There's just nothing more you can do.'

Colin's reluctance was not sentiment. His arms had become so stiff that he couldn't raise them sufficiently to exert any pressure on the girl's body. The committal was performed by Macdonald.

The woman the professor was supporting died too. But he had heard all that Colin had said, and he thought him the bravest and kindest boy he had ever known.

Everything in Third Officer Lee's boat had gone so smoothly to begin with that the shock when things went wrong had been doubly shattering. This boat, the farthest astern on the weather side, and the last to be lowered, had seemed to have every chance. The way on the ship had fallen right off, the launching crew had worked well together, and the boat had reached the promenade deck in good order. Just as Lee was looking forward to having a dry boat, the first setback came, as with nearly all the other boats, with the jamming of one of the falls. The occupants, who had originally included fifteen boys under Michael Rennie, had been catapulted into the sea. This was when Rennie had dived repeatedly to bring children back into what had become a waterlogged boat, its equipment either inaccessible or lost. It was largely due to Rennie that thirteen of the fifteen regained the boat.

Proudfoot, the barman, had entered this boat after the initial flooding, as had the German doctor Martin Bum.

Lee knew that an SOS had been sent and acknowledged, and he made sure for the sake of morale that all were aware of it, but he searched for distress rockets in vain. They too must have been spilled. All he had was a torch he had borrowed from Rennie.

It was soon apparent, to Lee and to others, that only a pick-up within a few hours would be effective in saving the children. To warm them up Rennie tried to get a sing-song going, but the response was depressingly feeble. Most of the boys had grabbed coats of some kind, but underneath they had nothing more substantial than pyjamas and life-jackets, and they were shivering with cold and shock from their ducking. Clenching their teeth to stop their jaws quivering put singing out of the question.

Proudfoot, sitting in the stern, thought what a tragedy it was that the boys hadn't slept in their clothes. That, he knew, had been the captain's orders, also the chief officer's, and he wondered who could have changed them. Someone must have concluded that the danger was over.

Lee, in the bows, knew that the buoyancy tanks would prevent the boat sinking, but he feared that it might overturn and directed his energies to preventing it from doing so. He also had an injured crewman to consider, and two injured children. The two male passengers, Bum and another man, would have to fend for themselves.

There were fifteen Lascars in this boat, and although they had worked well during the launching they quickly became docile if not apathetic. On the ship they had shown much attention and kindness to the evacuee children, but now they were too cold and miserable to do more than look after themselves. The feminine touch was also absent, there being no women in this boat. This left Proudfoot and the dynamic German doctor with the monosyllabic name as the only ones likely to give worth-while support to Rennie in encouraging and stimulating the children.

A witness of Rennie's life-saving marathon was Bess Walder's young brother, the eleven-year-old Louis. Already an admirer of the young theological student, he hero-worshipped him now. But as the storms raged over them and the swell engulfed them, nothing could reduce the depth of the flooding, and as in most boats the boys were immersed up to their waists and often their chests. Soon they were almost totally immobilized with stiffness and cramp. They continually saw lights, which they eagerly pointed out, but dejection always followed as the source was traced to some other lifeboat. Rennie assured them that help would be coming but he too was flagging, his energy so prodigally spent.

Proudfoot's height (six feet one inch) enabled him to keep two-thirds of his body clear of the water, but the proportion was halved for the children. He was nursing a boy who feared for the life of his sister; she had been in Sybil Gilliat-Smith's boat, from which he had seen half the complement pitched headlong into the sea. His name was Rex Thorne, of the Wembley group, and his sister was the enchanting seven-year-old Marion Thorne, better known as 'Mary for Short'. She had been among the group which had got separated from Mary Cornish, and sadly she had been one of the many girls lost in that ungovernable plunge. Proudfoot held the boy close, com-municating his own body warmth, but he thought the boy needed reviving and he produced the bottle of whisky he had so thoughtfully procured from the bar. After giving Rex Thorne a swig he handed it round.

For two or three hours the children kept up their spirits, determined not to let their guardian down after all he had done for them. The mouthful of whisky temporarily restored them, and Rennie, sitting amidships among them, signalled his appreciation to Proudfoot. It was not long afterwards, though, when the moon gave one of its fleeting peeps through the overcast, that Proudfoot met Rennie's gaze once again – and shuddered. It might be no more than a transient lapse, an unguarded moment of utter fatigue. But Proudfoot was sure it wasn't a trick of the light. Rennie's eyes were beginning to glaze.

Although still nursing a boy on each arm, Rennie was not far short of unconscious. Martin Bum noticed it too. 'Are you all right?' he asked Rennie. 'Yes, I'm all right, but I'm afraid I can't do much more.' He had worn himself out, but he added: 'I'm so glad to have you in the boat.'

Thus far, Bum had salvaged his much-treasured documents, but now, in order to work unencumbered to prevent the children from drifting away, he was obliged to discard them. There was no place to store them. It was a sacrifice he tried to forget. Meanwhile three children had actually drifted outside the boat and were floating in their life-jackets alongside; he struggled to pull them back in, but with no one to help but the other children he found it a strenuous task. The buoyancy of the life-jackets was one of the problems. Every time he managed to get a boy back to his seat or to a protected spot – as he thought – the next breaker lifted him out again.

The Lascars seemed not to understand a word that was spoken. The effect on them of the cold and immersion was complete stupefaction. They gave no trouble, but one by one they began to expire where they sat.

The boys too were much weaker now, hushed and immobile, and appalled by the change in Rennie. The two who had suffered injury – one had a fractured arm and the other concussion from a blow on the head – were the first to die.

A brave attempt by Rennie to regain control and assert himself ended in gibberish, and soon afterwards he died. The effect on the surviving children was calamitous, one boy crying piteously.

In the darkness Bum suddenly discovered that the heads of some of the boys were getting periodically swamped. Several were clinging together in the vain hope of finding a hold. It was impossible for Bum to help them all, but he extracted two of the younger ones. They were so sodden and limp that he passed them to Proudfoot in the stern, where they would be relatively safe – at least for a time.

Bum gave an Asian sitting beside him the task of holding one boy's head above water and he willingly tried it, but the task proved too much. The next time Bum looked, the boy's head had dropped and it was already too late.

An upturned boat drifted by with a man standing astride the keel and two girls (not Beth and Bess) apparently kneeling to keep their balance, one either side of the keel. They shouted and whistled, hoping to be taken aboard, and Lee would have welcomed them as additional help for the children. The man tried to impel the capsized boat towards them, but he made no progress, and without crew or oars Lee could do nothing. Still calling and whistling, they drifted despairingly away.

The man on the keel was Dubliner Maurice Maher, an oilfields superintendent, his original destination Venezuela. Told to jump for it when the ship sank, he had been one of those who swam to a waterlogged boat which then overturned. Clinging to the keel, he had been joined by an engineer and two teenage girls in their nightdresses.

Dragged back twice by Maher, the engineer had eventually slid out of reach. Now the lives of the two girls, both evacuees, were in jeopardy.

Maher had a coat under his life-jacket, and he was trying to get it off to give to the girls; this was why he was on his feet when he sighted Lee's boat. But owing to his precarious stance he found the contortions impossible. Neither of the girls survived the night.

As morning approached, Bum was holding on grimly and numbly to the five children remaining in his part of the boat. When daylight came Lee pointed out gently that all five were dead.

Everywhere it was the elderly, the very young, and the Lascars whose resistance proved weakest and who were the first to lose touch with reality. The two little evacuee boys in the Quintons' boat became drowsily lethargic and fell fast asleep almost unnoticed. They couldn't be roused. There was no one to mourn them, which rendered their deaths, after all that had happened, shockingly commonplace. Death had crept up on them and they had had nothing with which to resist it. Emma Guggenheim fell into a coma from which her husband revived her, but his own strength was faltering. Tony had thought that their well-covered frames, like his own and his mother's, must give them an advantage in circumstances like this over the lean and the weedy, but the Guggenheims were hardly supporting his theory. No doubt their ages – he was sixty-seven and she was fifty-nine – were against them. Forced flight from their homeland, too, could have affected their powers of resistance.

Before Emma recovered consciousness, Hirsch asked Szekulesz to look after his wallet; saturated though it was, it contained all his American securities and money. No sooner had Emma responded to her husband's ministrations, however, than Hirsch appeared to have a heart attack. Presently he died, and Emma's perplexity and grief were harrowing to watch. Indeed, after the unmourned passing of the children her wailing seemed almost immoderate. When she discovered that her husband's wallet was missing, and that Szekulesz had it, she asked for it back.

Hirsch had collapsed on his face, and she continued to hold on to him. Gripping the nape of his coat, she rocked him to and fro in the water in a rhythmic, sedative motion, as though even now she could communicate affection and comfort. As the action proved soothing to her, no one stopped her. Instead of looking macabre it seemed perfectly natural.

Later, in a moment of mental clarity, the poor woman sat up in horror, suddenly overwhelmed by her loss. Unable to face it, or at the end of her resources, she fell forward beside her husband and did not reappear.

Florence Croasdaile, too, was showing signs of derangement, and she was continually lamenting the plight of her children, both of whom had suffered immersion during the launching and were half-immersed now. To ease her in body and mind, the supernumerary chief engineer clasped the two-year-old boy under his jacket to generate warmth, and Szekulesz took charge of the girl.

Quartermaster Collin, the man who had been at the wheel when the ship was torpedoed, had thirty-three in his boat, including Arthur Wimperis, travel agent William Forsyth, escort Padre King, and twenty-one children – fifteen of King's group, the two quarantined boys and four stragglers rescued from the water. Gunner Harry Peard, for instance, in his search for what he felt would be a suitable berth for himself, had towed two children to this boat and cheerfully demanded 'Take these!'. Collin, like some others, was riding to a sea anchor, which he found effective in steadying the waterlogged boat. Most of the equipment was intact and there were ample emergency rations, but the blankets, which they wrapped round the children, were soon washed away. They were up to their armpits in water, baling was useless, and they were continually drenched by breakers and spray.

Wimperis and Forsyth found it maddeningly frustrating to watch the mounting death toll and be totally unable to check it. Even Collin could do nothing, and the night hours developed into a horrific saga of torture and misery. Forsyth was not a deeply religious man, but he shrank from the callousness of tipping the dead overboard without piety or prayer. Padre King himself was an early casualty, and Forsyth took over his role. As the children relinquished their hold on life he knelt in the water beside them, recited what he could remember of the service for committals at sea, then helped to slip them overboard with some show of reverence. This served a dual purpose, in that it also lightened the load and increased the chances of the living. There were some Lascars among them, but by far the majority of those whom he commended to the mercy of God were evacuee children.

Even in such dire adversity, a streak of grim humour persisted. Now that Forsyth could no longer plan people's travel in this world, suggested Wimperis, he was giving them tickets for the next.

One man who was resolving to voice his criticisms of the whole organization – if he survived – was the RNVR man Richard Deane. He had the right streak of ruthlessness for command in desperate circumstances, and the revolver to help him to assert it, but what angered and

frustrated him was what he saw as incompetence during
the launching and inadequacies in the lifeboat equipment.
Even when he finally got the Fleming gear fitted, he found
the handles too stiff to operate. Had they been readily
usable he believed his boat could have got away from the
ship's side without being flooded.

Accustomed as he was to storms in the Atlantic, he did
not rate this one as excessive. It was true that his had
been a weatherside boat, but had the launching gone
smoothly they would have shipped far less water – not
more, he believed, than might have been effectually baled
out. As it was, his role of lifeboat commander had been
aborted by circumstances beyond his control, and they
could do little but drift about broadside-on to the sea with
gunwales awash. The deaths that followed could not be
prevented; they were entirely due to exposure, immersion
and cold. The four Lascars who had joined the boat at the
last moment all perished, and a male passenger died soon
afterwards. Then, shortly before dawn, Deane's bitterness
was intensified by the death of his wife.

After drifting past Beth and Bess on their upturned boat,
Maud Hillman had clung to the two flaxen-haired Spencer
children for as long as she could. But eventually, either
unconscious or dead, they were washed off the raft.
Exhausted herself, and conscience-stricken, she lost contact with the raft in trying to save them. But she floated,
and not long afterwards she was picked out of the water
by Joe Hetherington and John Anderson, who were on a
much larger raft with eight others.

Throughout the night the chief officer and the purser
kept a 360-degree look-out for ships or a chance to get
into a lifeboat; they saw nothing of the former and only
the lights in the distance of the latter. Meanwhile they

were fully occupied in balancing the raft and maintaining their own places on it against the incessant pounding of ocean and the seething Atlantic gale. Gradually their shipmates were overcome, yet there was nothing they could do for them. They lost all their male companions, and long before morning the only remaining women were Maud Hillman and a tendentious but tenacious German/ Jewish refugee whose name they didn't know.

'Where is your famous British Navy?' demanded the German woman. 'Why haven't they come to rescue us?'

'What happened to your German Navy?' countered Hetherington. 'Why didn't they obey the code of the sea and care for survivors?'

The raft that the Brixton lad Jack Keeley was trying to reach after the sinking was the one which already supported Davis and McGlashan. He kept calling for help, but it was a long time before they heard his cries above the commotion of the elements. At last they spotted him, but to get him on to their tiny raft without capsizing it, especially with McGlashan almost prostrate with his head injury, posed problems. Dropping into the water, Davis decided to concentrate first on lifting the boy on to the raft. He was helping him up when a wave came along and completed the job for him. Then he clambered back himself.

The boy still had both life-jackets on, but nothing but pyjama-bottoms otherwise, and no coat. He was trying to speak through chattering teeth but making scarcely a sound. How much better his chances of survival would have been, thought Davis, if he had been properly clothed. Now, crouched on all fours, clutching the slats for support, he was still choking and gasping for breath. The two men wondered what message he could possibly have that he felt so important to deliver. But he was only minding his manners. 'I say . . . I say . . . thanks very much.'

With twenty-foot waves smashing over the top of this six-feet-by-three platform and exploding beneath them to burst through the slats, it was hard for the three to keep station. The boy especially was in constant danger, even though they placed him in the middle, and for much of the time they lay virtually on top of him, anchoring him to the raft and keeping the wind off him too. In rapid succession they would climb to the top of a wave, plunge into the trough, and then soar to the top again, wondering each time if the next trough would capsize them. But the boy had recovered his voice, he was not seasick and he chattered away continually. Davis didn't think for one moment of trying to stop him. It kept the boy awake, and even perhaps helped keep him warm.

The provisions on this raft, stored in a watertight locker, included canned milk, ships' biscuits, and water. There was even a can-opener, and Davis tried opening some milk, but passing the tin round on their helter-skelter of a craft called for trapeze-artiste balance quite beyond BBC training. When one can was swept away, they saved the others for emergencies. They were not yet in need of it, but the time would probably come.

Worst of all for them, Davis felt, was their complete ignorance of what rescue operations were in progress. To have had some idea of how long their ordeal might last – to be able to pace themselves – would give them a target to aim at and help them endure.

The boy never whimpered, but he asked many questions. He was worried about his six-year-old sister Joyce. Did Davis think she was all right? She would have been looked after by Aunt Mary, wasn't that so?

Davis did not discourage the boy in his optimism. But unknown to them both, the girl had been spilled out of one of the boats, and she was not seen again.

When Marguerite Bech, with Sonia and Derek, tried to lie down on their raft to rest, the seas covered their faces; when they sat up, they were blown down again by the gale. Still with them were the Australian nurse Doris Walker and the young seventh engineer Tommy Milligan. Initially Marguerite's greatest concern was for Barbara; so far as she knew, Barbara had gone down that rope ladder and been mauled by the sea. In the darkness and chaos, Derek had not seen whether she had reached the boat safely or not.

In fact, Barbara's boat, No. 4, with thirty-three people on board, nineteen of them Lascars, was in far better shape than the others, having escaped flooding at the launching. One other boat had done equally well, No. 12, but that boat had vanished. No one had seen anything of it since the sinking, and the fear was that some unforeseen catastrophe had overtaken it. In Boat 4, however, where crewmen McEwan and McAlister had put out a sea anchor, as Collin had done, the craft was kept head-on to the waves and there seemed no danger that it would broach to or capsize. The Fleming gear worked satisfactorily, regular baling kept the water down to six or eight inches, the boat had a hood, and although the seas still broke over their heads this gave them useful protection from the wind. Thus a seaworthy state was maintained. Being unflooded they had no trouble finding the rations, and a twenty-four-year-old Canadian girl named Peggy Ducker, calm and phlegmatic, took over the provisioning, assisted by the Choat family (minus Frank, who was missing). There was plenty of milk, biscuits and brandy, and twelve blankets to share.

There were no child evacuees in this boat – it was one of the forward boats, the second on the port or lee side – and Barbara Bech was the youngest. All the Europeans were properly clothed, but the Lascars, having responded well during the launching, suffered far greater physical degeneration than the Europeans through exposure and their own scanty clothing. They became increasingly introverted and listless, losing interest in the routine of running the boat and leaving the baling to others. Yet none as yet betrayed any signs of mortal distress. Thus both Europeans and Asians were proving the point made by Deane in Boat 7 – that if the boats could have been launched without flooding, and if the equipment had not been saturated or missing, none of the incidents that had so tragically depleted their numbers need have occurred.

No such judgements were available to those stranded on rafts, like the three Bechs. Pummelled by sledgehammer seas, they feared many times that their craft must capsize. Twice Sonia was prised from her hold, and each time Marguerite despaired of her rescue. The second time Sonia despaired too, though dispassionately, giving herself up with calm resignation. As the ocean closed over her and she somersaulted down, eardrums stunned and hearing attenuated, she experienced a surge of serenity. The thunder of the elements was suddenly inaudible, replaced by a soporific hum. Torn from her precarious perch, irrevocably as it seemed, she almost welcomed oblivion. With a childlike faith in immortality, she wondered what God would be like.

She had reckoned without Tommy Milligan. The nineteen-year-old engineer seized her as she surfaced and hauled her back on to the raft.

* * *

After their disappointment at the failure of the flooded lifeboat to reach them, Beth and Bess, still on the upturned boat, suffered a sag in morale. Keeping their eyes tightly shut to protect them from the salty sting of the breakers, they hardly noticed that their company was beginning to dwindle, until only two Lascars remained. Even these two seemed half crazed by cold and despair. When did the darkness end in these waters? The night stretched interminably ahead, and each of the girls experienced moments of abject depression when their natural ebullience deserted them and they felt like loosening their hold. What was the use? The only thing that sustained them, in these low moments, was the instinctive knowledge – they did not discuss it – that if one surrendered to the temptation, so would the other. Their lives had become interdependent. What kept them going was companionship; they owed it to each other not to give in.

Another blessing was the illusion that the convoy was still in attendance and would pick them up in the morning. The letdown, when it came, might bring dejection, but it was all they had to buoy up their hopes through the night. That the vessels they had sailed alongside for four days might abandon them to their fate did not seem credible. Hold on till daylight! That was their goal, that was what they told themselves, over and over again. If they could do that, rescue would come.

It was not, in fact, solely a question of holding on. As the upturned boat rose on the crests, their bodies rose with it; but when it toppled into the trough their bodies were momentarily suspended in mid-air until gravity reasserted itself and they came down on the boat with a thud, squeezing their life-jackets into their chests. The clinker-built boat was not a smooth surface, and they were continually battered and bruised and sometimes winded as well.

Occasionally they caught snatches of speech, unintelligible to them, from the Lascars, but they guessed from the tone that they were praying. No one, thought Beth, could be praying harder than she was.

Hour after hour they held on, until they seemed to have been rising and falling on that capricious surface for days. But at last they saw something that lifted their spirits. Doubtful at first, and disbelieving each other, they stared bleary-eyed at the eastern sky. At length there was no doubt about it: the first streaks on the horizon foreshadowed the approach of the day. Never had they experienced a more merciful dawn.

Dimly now they could discern the silhouette of the two Lascars, and they turned to look at them, to commiserate and encourage, and perhaps to draw from their strength. One of them, mentally deranged, was alternately muttering and laughing. The other was silent. In the half-light they saw that to stop himself falling off he had lashed himself to the propeller. Even on that vantage point, well clear of the sea, spray and spume were continually crashing over his head.

A marginal increase in light and they were able to confirm their suspicions. The man's head, dripping with water from each inundation, hung limp, as though his neck had been broken. He had long since been dead.

Averting their gaze, they turned eagerly to scan the horizon as full daylight drew near. Expecting to see many ships, they detected nothing but featureless ocean. They blinked with incredulity. This could not be. An unbroken horizon encircled them, and they gazed until ocean and sky seemed to merge.

There was not so much as a lifeboat in sight, nor even

a raft. Nothing. Nothing but sea. Thus, with a dead man and a madman for company, they faced the long-awaited new day.

In the breasts of all the survivors, in that chill, anti-climactic moment, despondency reigned. Hopeless and helpless, abandoned and betrayed, each withdrew into his or her own personal despair.

6
'Why Don't You Pray?'

Battering her way through a Force 9 gale and a tempestuous sea, tossing and pitching, swaying and shuddering, HMS *Hurricane* progressed at a speed of 15 knots towards the mid-Atlantic, shaping a course roughly westwards of 286 degrees, aiming for the position given by C.-in-C. Western Approaches. No one yet knew the extent of the tragedy, but Lieutenant-Commander Simms had been left in no doubt that his mission was urgent. 'Utmost despatch' was enough. Yet the elements combined to hamper and handicap. Riding the hammer-blows of ocean and gale at a maximum speed consistent with the safety of his ship, he was forced to exercise what patience he could. At their present rate he could not hope to reach the survivors, whoever they were, before mid-afternoon. Meanwhile, in consultation with his navigation officer, Lieutenant Pat Fletcher, he worked out a likely search area.

In boats as on rafts, full daylight sharpened both vision and dread. Soon the seascape, revealed briefly in all its desolation, was obliterated by a bombardment of hailstones and sleet more savage than anything suffered before. So brutal was the assault that depleted boat crews were hard put to it to keep their craft from capsizing.

In most boats, some effort was made to disgorge the night's dead; though not all boats had survivors able to do it.

Marjorie Day's lifeboat was roughly in the centre of the ravaged flotilla. None of the boats was within hailing distance, yet she thought she counted twelve including her own. They were scattered around her in a wide radius, as far as the eye could see, and three were upturned. But the dispersal and isolation that seemed certain to follow had not yet occurred.

Her reckoning was wrong in one respect only. There were indeed twelve boats afloat and in view, but one was from the freighter *Marina*, torpedoed soon after the *Benares*. The liner's twelfth boat – it had been the farthest astern on the port side, Ronnie Cooper's boat, Boat 12 – was still missing.

For some of the boats on the outer perimeter, the reassurance of seeing other boats was lacking. Alex Macauley, who had lost ten of his Lascars (though not the indomitable deck serang) during the night, and one of the two Jewish refugees he had saved at the time of the sinking, saw nothing of his shipwrecked colleagues when daylight came, though he was assured by the deck serang that lights had been visible until just before dawn. Oil on the water, too, suggested they were not far from the spot where the vessel went down.

When the storm eventually abated, a bright sunshine broke through, bringing some lifting of spirits. Those with the strength left to care felt hungry or thirsty, and by rummaging about in the flooded lockers and in the bilges, sustenance was found. Tins of corned beef and condensed milk, and packets of ships' biscuits, were discovered and opened with various implements, but many mouths were too swollen and dry for full mastication. The heavily sweetened milk, however, tasted like nectar, and in one boat there was enough for every occupant to have his or her own tin. The Lascars, too, ate and drank eagerly. Water was either missing or polluted by sea water, but

1 a *above* The SS *City of Benares*
  b *left* John Anderson
  c *below* Captain Landles Nicoll
  d *foot* Joe Hetherington

2 a *above* The Grimmond sisters – Violet, Gussie and Connie

  b *below left* Rosemary Spencer-Davies

  c *below right* John Spencer-Davies

a *above* Florence Croasdaile on Bournemouth
beach with Lawrence and Patricia, 1939

b *below right* Michael Rennie

c *below left* Mary Cornish

4 a *above left* Kapitänleutnant Heinrich Bleichrodt, commander of *U48*

b *above right* Lt-Cdr Hugh Crofton Simms, commander of HMS *Hurricane*

c *below left* Henry and Phyllis Digby-Morton

d *below right* Johnny Baker, Rex Thorne and Jack Keeley

5 a *above* Bess Walder

b *left* Beth Cummings

c *below* Colin Ryder Richardson (centre) with Sonia and Derek Bech

6 a *top* An RAF Sunderland flying-boat circling the missing Boat 12

b *above* The survivors (taken from HMS *Anthony*)

7 a *top* The moment of rescue

b *above* Five of Mary Cornish's boys with HMS *Anthony* crew members

8 Friends and neighbours turn out
  to greet Kenneth Sparks at Wembley

most boats, and even some rafts, had brandy or rum. Yet every hour brought further fatalities.

In Third Officer Lee's boat some extra blankets were found, which were shared between children and Lascars, but in their soaked condition they gave little comfort. Of more value was a tarpaulin, which was erected over the stern.

In Angus Macdonald's boat, a young man who had shared Colin's cabin on the ship lost his reason when daylight found them deserted, and he threatened to throw them all out of the boat before killing himself. Macdonald pacified and restrained him, but later, after shouting abuse at the empty horizon, he flung himself overboard. Twice Macdonald retrieved him but the third time he sank out of sight.

One woman in this boat deliberately entangled her legs round an iron bar so that she couldn't be swept overboard. Professor Day, feeling the onset of delirium, jammed his legs under the mast, which lay horizontally inside the boat. Colin was still well covered, but his balaclava had slipped round the back of his neck and he couldn't raise his arms to pull it straight.

Haunted by the ghastly succession of committals during the night, William Forsyth cooperated in tying the remaining boys in his boat – one was John Baker, another was Alan Capel – to the thwarts in a sitting position, using sacking they found in the boat. Quartermaster Collin remained in control in this boat, but Forsyth was wilting.

Seven of the children in Third Officer Lee's boat had perished during the night, together with an equal number of Lascars. Their bodies were lifted overboard by Lee, the swirling water in the boat easing his task. This was the boat in which everyone was given a tin of condensed milk. But by midday, four more of the children and one more

Lascar were dead. That left, of the children in the boat, only Rex Thorne and Louis Walder. If rescue didn't come soon, there would be no child survivors at all.

All would be mourned, but none more so than the next girl to die in Boat 10. After all she had done for the younger children, on the ship and for hour after hour in the lifeboat, and with the arrival of help surely imminent, the slender and talented Rosemary Spencer-Davies was the next to succumb. Rosemary never knew it, but her young brother John had perished already.

The only child still alive in this boat was the Sunderland girl Eleanor Wright. Marjorie Day, watching her closely, thought that only an immense vitality, coupled with exceptional will-power, kept her going. Her faith in rescue was undiminished. 'Don't worry,' she told her grown-up companions, 'the Navy won't let us down.'

Florence Croasdaile's two children, Patricia and Lawrence, were still alive at daybreak, thanks to the two men who nursed them, Ernest Szekulesz and the supernumerary chief engineer. In this boat the man who found and dispensed the provisions was Tony Quinton's Lascar friend Gunga Din; he opened the tins, handed them round and continued to be the most active man in the boat. But two more passengers died, and the American woman was only subconsciously aware of her surroundings. In her wanderings she talked of her children, calling repeatedly for Lawrence, who at two years old was little more than a baby in arms. 'My baby, my baby!' she moaned. The two men, by mutual agreement, signalled that both children were all right, and the engineer pretended to feed the baby from a milk tin. But the drop in temperature during the early-morning hailstorm had penetrated what little protection the two men could give. Both children were dead, but the

men continued to nurse them, hiding the truth from the
mother, shielding their bodies long after life had departed.
Later that morning the mother died too, without knowing
the fate of her children.

Deane found when the sun rose that his boat was
colliding with wreckage. They were drifting through a
river of lumber, mostly planks from the deck cargo of the
Marina. This gave him an idea. Under his guidance they
shipped three of these planks and placed them athwart-
ships over the gunwales. This gave his complement something to sit on clear of the water. It was a life-saving ploy,
and it galled him to think that it had come too late to save
his wife. Preserving the balance of the boat became more
critical, but the state of those who had survived this far
perceptibly improved. Whether it would do more than
prolong the agony he could not tell; he had confidently
forecast that rescue would come at first light.

In the course of the morning, as they see-sawed incessantly on the swell, Beth and Bess caught a glimpse of a
clutter of flotsam, or so it appeared, some distance away.
It turned out to be a lifeboat, with people in it, fully
seaworthy it seemed, with plenty of freeboard. They at
once started shouting, but their throats were so shrivelled
by salt that their voices were muffled and hoarse, and
they knew they wouldn't be heard. But in time they were
sighted – by none other than Barbara Bech in the
unflooded Boat 4. McVicar and McAlister got the Fleming gear going, and they were close enough for Barbara
to identify four figures on the upturned boat, two European girls of about her own age, and two Lascars, one
whose head was lolling and who was pretty obviously
dead. But reaching them, in seas of frustrating antagon-
ism, was proving too much for the two seamen. They also

realized that they were courting disaster: the harder they worked the handles, and the more help they got from their complement, the greater the danger became of broaching to and capsizing.

Beth and Bess saw their struggles only fleetingly, when the crests coincided, and it was some time before they realized that vigorous effort had ceased and the boat was drifting away. Dismayed and despondent, they were ready to give themselves up to the sea. Yet their fingers were frozen round the rope in a death-grip, and whether they wished to or not it seemed that they couldn't leave go.

Only their imaginations sustained them now. They pictured their homes, their loved ones, their school-friends, and visualized how, at this very moment, in the old familiar classrooms, their teachers would be taking the lessons. Beth felt herself back in the strangely scented atmosphere of day-school, and both girls found their reveries gave them real comfort. Bess had a focus on which to keep her mind working throughout – her worries about Louis, and whether he had survived in his lifeboat. She knew nothing of his rescue by the Sunderland boy George Crawford, or of the sacrificial devotion of Michael Rennie, but her interest in her brother's fate was intense. She felt she must know, and it stiffened her will to survive.

They tried to talk to each other, but their senses were atrophied, and even at point-blank range their croaks were inaudible. Beth was fascinated to see huge blocks of ice floating around her and giant fish leaping above her, though even as she witnessed these wonders she knew they must be hallucinations. Consciousness returned when another gigantic sea choked her and left her coughing and spluttering, eyes smarting and hearing benumbed. But neither girl felt pain any more.

Whereas the night had seemed interminably long, the

day was frighteningly short, creeping towards afternoon and a lowering sun with incredible speed. What would they do if they weren't found before dark? They would never live through another night.

On the raft holding Joe Hetherington and John Anderson, Maud Hillman died and they were using her corpse as a windbreak. The German woman was alternately quarrelsome and insensible, and many times they had to prevent her from slipping and sliding into the sea. They were exhausting themselves in their efforts to save her. Why not dump her? It would be much easier to keep the raft balanced without her. Then in their semi-delirium they noticed she was wearing a tartan scarf, brightly colourful against their own nondescript clothing. 'That scarf might be useful to signal with,' said Hetherington. 'It might save our lives.' Certainly it saved the German woman at that moment. It was part of the two men's mental derangement that, having considered an act that bordered on murder, they did not even think of getting rid of the body and retaining the scarf.

Their bizarre conversation was conducted in the woman's hearing, with no attempt at concealment, and she seemed to divine their intention. Suddenly she revived for a moment and spoke much more calmly. 'Why don't you pray?'

'Me?' queried Anderson. 'I wouldn't know what to pray about.' But the woman persisted, perhaps aware that murder and prayer might not mix, and together the three of them, haltingly but accurately, recited the Lord's Prayer.

When they opened their eyes it seemed that their prayer had been answered. The shout came from Hetherington. 'I saw a ship!'

Whatever it was that Hetherington had seen was

instantly masked by intervening crests, and Anderson, who did not have the advantage of the chief officer's great height, was sceptical. They were all beginning to hallucinate. 'You're seeing things, Joe,' said Anderson. Meanwhile the German woman, afraid to believe it was true, turned to ridicule. A three-cornered quarrel developed, and eventually Hetherington, having stood up on the raft and waved a handkerchief in his excitement, slowly conceded that he might have been the victim of an optical illusion. As the hours passed and he saw nothing more, he came to believe it.

Eric Davis shared the general experience of scanning the horizon at sunrise in vain. Then came the hailstones, and he almost despaired. He still believed he could endure much longer if he only knew that rescue was coming. Even when the weather brightened for a time the seascape was bare. Surely there must be planes out there somewhere, searching for them. A plane might not be able to help them directly, but the sight of one would have raised their morale and given them courage. The only things airborne around them that morning were seagulls.

To cheer themselves up they had breakfast. McGlashan, still half bemused, ate and drank little, but whenever Davis gave biscuits to Jack Keeley he ate them, when told to drink the condensed milk he drank it, and when the hailstorms had passed he nattered away as before. 'Sir,' he asked, 'which way are we going?'

'*That* way,' said Davis, pointing. 'The wind is blowing us that way.'

'Yes,' said Keeley, 'but which way is that? Are we still going to Canada, or are we on our way back to England?'

Clearly the boy had no idea what such voyages entailed,

and Davis did not enlighten him. 'Back to England, I should think.' With this the boy seemed satisfied.

They were still swamped at intervals, and on this tiny raft they still had to be careful not to fall off. One or other of them was continually on the point of slithering into the water, and they rearranged themselves every few minutes. To try to keep warm, and to fend off cramp, Davis encouraged the boy to join him in simple exercises, raising and lowering arms and legs and flexing muscles. McGlashan twisted and turned, but that was in semi-delirium; otherwise, conserving his strength, he lay doggo. Lightly built though the engineer was, he was obviously wiry, decided Davis, or he wouldn't have lasted so long.

Every smudge of cloud deceived them into detecting phantom ships, and it was Keeley who kept up their spirits. At midday he and Davis amused themselves by throwing biscuit crumbs to the gulls, but during the afternoon the boy at last quietened down. He had almost dozed off when he suddenly pulled at Davis's arm.

'Look – look at him! Quick!'

The boy was the first to react. McGlashan was slipping off the raft. Between them they grabbed him and fiercely held on, dragging him back inch by inch. Davis shook him and slapped him to restore his awareness when they got him back on, then worked out a fresh intertwining of limbs which virtually bound them together.

Davis did not think they would ever have saved McGlashan once he had gone. He owed his life to the boy.

Keeley's questions now became slightly light-headed. 'How do you stop these things,' he asked, 'when you want to get off?' As the juvenile chatter became spasmodic and inconsequential, Davis's anxiety increased.

The afternoon light was palpably waning, the wind was freshening, the seas were burgeoning, and the gulls had gone. A storm before sunset looked likely. That, surely, would destroy any chance of a rescue. Could they conceivably last a second night? Davis doubted it. He regretted the few crumbs of biscuit they'd thrown to the gulls, and he ruled out any further intake of milk before dusk. They were down to their very last tin.

By mid-morning Marguerite Bech had begun to give up hope. The empty canisters that gave the raft buoyancy were loosening, and their hands, as they tried to retain their grip on the slats, were torn and bleeding. If the raft disintegrated, as it seemed likely to do, they were finished.

If rescue were coming it would have reached them by now: that, overcome by tedium and fatigue, was Marguerite's conclusion. 'Sonia darling,' she said, 'I think we'll just take off our lifebelts and go to sleep in the water.' Earlier Sonia had resigned herself to death; now she demurred. 'Oh no, Mummy, don't do that. I'm sure we'll be picked up soon.'

Miraculously, Sonia was right. Almost in that moment, to their incredulous joy, some sort of yacht, sails flapping, hove into view. It was circling at a distance, as though sizing them up, and they shouted and waved frantically for help. The 'yacht' proved to be one of *Marina*'s two lifeboats, with the second officer in charge. Both the freighter's boats had been launched without flooding, and during the night they had spread their sails over themselves for protection. At dawn they had hoisted them independently and steered a south-easterly course, making for the Northern Irish coast, a voyage of some 650 miles. They thought they could make it in about a week if the winds remained westerly. The captain's boat was nowhere in sight, but this boat picked up the Bechs – Marguerite, Sonia and Derek – the Australian Doris Walker and Tommy Milligan, the seventh engineer. After rescuing three more survivors, all Lascars, from another raft, they resumed their voyage.

When Marguerite Bech learned what lay ahead of them, incredulity returned, but with dismay now rather than joy. She wondered if they hadn't exchanged the frying-pan for the fire.

By ten past eight that morning the elements had moderated sufficiently for Lieutenant-Commander Simms to increase speed to 27 knots, bringing his estimated time of arrival at the scene of the sinking several hours forward. At 10.00, when the wind veered to the south-west, he and Pat Fletcher, together on the bridge, resolved to approach to a point thirty miles east-north-east of the grave of the *Benares*. That way they would start their sweep upwind and sea, greatly reducing if not obviating the risk of missing craft driven downwind.

Three and a half hours later, at 13.30, they reached their preselected position, reduced speed and ordered every man not on duty, and many who were, to keep a look-out. Then they started their search. After forty-five minutes, at 14.15, when still fourteen miles from the position they'd been given of the sinking, they sighted a lifeboat. It seemed to be doing uncommonly well, scudding along under full sail. It was one of the lifeboats of the *Marina*.

This was the boat that, not very much earlier, had picked up the Bechs. When the occupants saw the destroyer they stood up and cheered, none more emotionally, and certainly none more groggily, than the

Bechs and their all-night companions. Nets were put down and the men of the *Marina* climbed them readily, but the five *Benares* survivors had to be helped up the ropes. After being force-fed with a calorific beverage called rum, they were sent below for hot drinks and hot baths. Meanwhile the Bechs were condemned to an agonized wait for news about Barbara.

The search was continued to windward and at 15.15 four tiny rafts were sighted, each with a single occupant. After plotting the various positions they made for the nearest. It hardly seemed possible for anyone to cling to it and survive, flung as it was from wave-top to wave-top as though in some savage end-to-end game. On it sat a dark-skinned man, turbaned and cross-legged, who contrived to wave to them feebly.

It was necessary for *Hurricane* to go alongside each raft, and the swell that was running complicated the task of recovering survivors and made each raft difficult to locate. The survivors, all Lascars, were exhausted and frozen, unlike the crew of the *Marina*, and they had to be hauled on board by running bowlines secured under their arms. Thus it was not until 15.53 that the four Lascars were safely extracted and the search was continued.

These light-weight rafts had been blown to the perimeter of the selected search area; but two miles further on, as *Hurricane* proceeded upwind, her siren sounding insistently, the first of the *Benares*' lifeboats was seen, then another and another. All but one were either capsized or waterlogged, and all but one contained no more than a handful of survivors. The exception was a boat which looked sound and seaworthy and more or less full. There were also several more rafts.

At length, having fixed the coordinates of their box search and taken the precaution of plotting all visible craft, Simms moved cautiously in. He and his crew had no conception of what they were about to discover.

'Look! A ship!'

Tony Quinton, hearing his mother's excited shout, turned to look where she was pointing and was just in time to glimpse the silhouette of a warship before the swell snatched it from view. But excitement turned to mild dismay when, next time they rose to a crest, the ship seemed to be heading away from them. 'They haven't seen us,' said Szekulesz, pessimistic as always. 'They will not come for us now. We are lost.' This brought out the best in Letitia Quinton. 'Nonsense.' The Hungarian spoke good English, but with an accent, and this led the lady to emphasize her point in a stilted but imperious vernacular. 'The big ship will come!'

The faithful tindal Gunga Din echoed this in an abbreviated vernacular of his own. 'Yes!' he confirmed. 'Big ship come!'

Soon afterwards Eric Davis heard hooting, but he ignored it. He had heard too many hooters already. As before, it could be nothing more than the clash of the breakers and the whine of the south-westerly wind. But McGlashan, silent and comatose for some hours, came to life at the sound. No seaman could mistake it. He sat up bemusedly, spotted one mast and then two, and announced: 'It's a destroyer!'

The ship was some distance off, and they knew they wouldn't be heard, but they yelled and shouted just the same. The vessel turned stern-on before swinging round and edging towards them. A rope was thrown, and it missed, but it was hauled back and thrown again. This time it was accurate, hitting Davis in the face. He was just in time to recover from the shock of the blow and hang on.

Jack Keeley could no longer stand, but Davis supported him and dragged him to his feet. Next time the raft rose on the swell almost to deck level the sailors managed to grab the boy and swing him aboard by an arm and a leg. In doing so they upset the balance of the raft and capsized it, tipping Davis and McGlashan into the sea. Sailors came down on running bowlines to fish them out, and they joined Keeley on board. A slug of rum was produced for Davis and McGlashan and hot milk for Keeley, but Davis felt that the boy, having stood up to the ordeal like a man, deserved a man's reward. 'Try a drop of this,' he said, and poured half his rum into the milk. After gulping it down with apparent relish, Keeley repeated the remark he had made at their first meeting more than sixteen hours ago, half choked and spluttering now as he had been then, though for a different reason. 'I say,' he said, 'I say . . . thanks very much.'

The incident persuaded Simms to put down a long-boat to pick up those on rafts and on upturned boats, and at 15.30 the long-boat passed right by the Quintons' boat, but disappointingly did not stop. 'We're picking people up from rafts at the moment,' said one of the crew, 'but we'll come back for you. Or rather, the destroyer itself will come for you soon.'

This sounded sensible enough to the Quintons. It was a moot point whether those on rafts were more exposed than those in boats, but it was an understandable priority. However, the promise did not appease Ernest Szekulesz. '*That is what they say*.'

After hoisting the long-boat, the destroyer moved on to rescue the survivors from Deane's boat, putting down nets for those able to claw their way up, and sending down sailors with bowlines for those who could not. The planking had protected the remainder of Deane's complement so well that no one had died in this boat since first light. Since seven had perished during the night, and as many Lascars, many of the sixteen who survived in this boat owed their lives to Deane's improvisation.

It now became a race against time to pick up the remaining survivors before dark. Yet only a methodical probing of the search area, lasting some hours, could make reasonably sure that no one was missed.

For Simms and Fletcher the plot they had made dictated their sequence. After dealing with most of the rafts, they picked off the boats as they came to them. They could not differentiate: one boat to them was the same as another. And indeed in all boats there were lives that hung by a thread.

Third Officer Lee's boat was next. Of its original thirty-four, fourteen were alive. Despite all the efforts, first of Rennie and then of Bum, Proudfoot and Lee, thirteen of the fifteen children had died. But Rex Thorne and Louis Walder were still alive when *Hurricane* manoeuvred alongside. The comparative vulnerability of the Asians as against the Europeans was amply demonstrated in this boat, where all the European men except Rennie survived but seven Asians perished. Paradoxically, though, it was the surviving Asians who had husbanded their strength sufficiently to climb up the nets of the destroyer, whereas Martin Bum was too weak to stand and had to be hauled on board after the children.

Boat 4, in which all thirty-three had survived, was reached just on 17.00. A cruel fate had ordained that none of the evacuee children was earmarked for this boat. The *Hurricane* crew, badgered by Marguerite Bech to ask for Barbara in each boat, found a fourteen-year-old girl in this one who answered to the description – and to the name. 'Your mother's been worried about you,' she was told. Not one-tenth as worried, thought Barbara, as I've been about them. The Bechs were the only complete family to survive so far; the Choats were in this boat – Sylvia and her three teenage children, Rachel, Peter and Russell – but Frank Choat was still missing.

Next it was the turn of the Quintons, and those of their companions who had survived. Szekulesz was gloomily forecasting some last-minute betrayal right to the end. Yet for all his pessimism he had been one of the stalwarts in this boat, giving practical help to others whenever he could. And he never stopped singing the praises of James Baldwin-Webb for his selfless work in assembling passengers and supervising the launching of the boat. Others who survived in this boat included Tony Quinton's pipe-smoking Priestley-type Yorkshireman and his two nick-named Lascars, Gunga Din and Basil Rathbone.

From the top of a high sea, Alex Macauley sighted two boats and two rafts at about noon and felt he was no longer alone. His was the next boatload to be picked up. Boatload was a misnomer: only Macauley – still wearing his cap – and three others (two Lascars and a Jewish refugee) had survived. Rescuers had to fix ropes round them to get them aboard.

Beth Cummings had hardly absorbed the fact that the light was beginning to fail when she heard Bessie shout. Silhouetted against the horizon was a ship, a real live ship, unmistakably a warship, so close and so three-dimensional that it could not be a delusion. But would they see the upturned boat, protruding so little from the swell, with even that little half-flooded for much of the time? Beth too tried to shout, but their croaks were scarcely audible even to themselves. They lacked the strength to wave, and in any case their hands were immutably locked round the rope. The ship seemed to be zigzagging, but it was definitely coming their way. Was it really coming for *them*?

Suddenly, as it towered above them, all doubts were dispersed. 'Thank God,' murmured Beth; she had never stopped praying. Simms brought his ship as near as he dared, and then the girls saw some liquid being poured overboard. They had no idea what it was. In fact it was oil, to temper the swell. They saw the crew lowering the long-boat, and then Beth passed out. The next thing she knew she was sitting in the boat with a sailor supporting her, with Bess sitting opposite, also in the care of a sailor. Then reaction set in. The sailors began to massage their limbs, two other sailors took their coats off to wrap round them, and the girls tried to smile at their jokes. But their expressions seized up: they were totally spent. How the sailors had loosened their death-grip they never discovered. Neither could spread her fingers for days.

When the boat was hoisted to deck level, a crowd of cheery faces gave them a welcome. Then it was rum, hot soup and a hot bath. The rum burnt their insides and the hot bath was torture as their limbs came back to life. But the Turkish towelling that dried them, and the sheets they slipped between in the first lieutenant's cabin, were luxuries beyond all imagining.

The second Lascar, although unconscious, was also rescued. When he recovered he said he owed his life to the girls. He would have given up hope without them.

Sole survivors on two other upturned boats, Dubliner Maurice Maher and naval signaller Micky Goy, were picked up by the long-boat soon afterwards. Maher could recall little of his experience, but Goy, who like the other

members of Mackinnon's staff had helped to launch rafts
and been among the last to leave the ship, remembered
that the ordeal of the night hours left only three of his
companions alive, a woman and two Lascars. Soon after
dawn the woman died in his arms, and one by one the
Lascars slid into the water.

A third upturned boat was found abandoned and
empty. Those who had clung to it had long since
succumbed.

In Marjorie Day's boat the crew used an oar to hoist the
pyjamas of a dead child to attract attention. This boat was
not reached until 18.40; meanwhile some of the occupants
felt faint with hunger. While the crew were rummaging
for food, Eleanor Wright, the last surviving child evacuee
out of fifteen in this boat, and the last of the Sunderland
girls who had formed such a happy party when they
started out a week earlier, volunteered to hold up the
flag. The sailors were reluctant at first to trust the flag to
her. 'Don't lose it, miss,' they said, 'without that they
may not find us.' She held it aloft steadily for some
minutes, until the wallowing lifeboat pitched her off her
balance and she fell, still clutching the makeshift flagstaff.
She was barely conscious, and close to final collapse,
when she and her companions were rescued.

It was 19.00 when they got to Angus Macdonald's boat,
where again hands had to go down on running bowlines
as the survivors were too far gone to help themselves.
Colin was the first to be hoisted, but then, left to himself
on deck for a moment while others were dealt with, he
collapsed and injured his head. Professor Day was taken
aboard unconscious, but his first question, after a tumbler
of rum had been poured down his throat to revive him,
concerned Colin. 'Is Colin all right?' When told that he

was, his relief was immense. 'That's done me more good than anything else,' he said, 'even the rum.' Pat Bulmer, too, survived, thanks to the dedicated nursing of Phyllis Digby-Morton.

Surgeon-Lieutenant Collinson was busy patching up survivors when an attractive woman, who had already acquired some dry clothes, came up to him and asked: 'Can I help?' Intent on his task, he did not realize at first that she was a survivor from a waterlogged boat. It was nearly an hour later when he noticed how pale she looked. 'Would you mind if I lay down for a little?' she asked. It was Phyllis Digby-Morton. How short-sighted he must have been, thought Collinson – and what an incredible girl.

William Forsyth had committed seventeen children to the deep by the time rescue came, but four boys were still breathing, though their lives hung by a thread. They were strapped to the thwarts to prevent them being flushed out. One was Johnny Baker, and he struggled fiercely to escape from his straitjacket as rescue began, fearful of being left behind. The others were comatose. Despite his sixty-five years, Arthur Wimperis also survived in this boat. But one of the boys in a coma, Alan Capel, who had got this far only through the devoted attentions of Dr Bum, died on the destroyer at the moment of rescue. (His brother Derek, who had been so concerned for his safety, had embarked in the missing Boat 12.)

Peter Collinson went to work at once on resuscitating the other two, both aged ten. They were Derek Carr, like Johnny Baker from Southall, and Terence Holmes, from Wembley.

The scenes on and around the destroyer as the light faded were phantasmagoric, a tableau of heroism, happiness, hysteria and horror. The waterlogged boats contained many women and children for whom rescue had come far too late, confronting the *Hurricane* crewmen, as they swung to the rescue, with scenes unimaginably macabre. In one boat there were four living and twenty-one dead.

While performing miracles of gallantry and deliverance, sailors toughened by twelve months of war were torn between cursing the Germans for this senseless slaughter and crying unashamedly at the sight.

By 19.30 the four-square-mile area of the destroyer's box search, punctiliously combed, was murky with dusk, and a grey overcast deepened the gloom. Yet Simms was determined that the quest should go on at least till last light. And on the far perimeter, a raft still supported two men and a woman. The men – Joe Hetherington and John Anderson – had agreed that darkness would be a sentence of death. They could not last another night. Already they were drowsy and lethargic, while the German woman, now comatose, no longer taunted them. Anderson was ready to give up, but Hetherington rebuked him. 'Think about your wife and the girls.' Then Anderson, like Hetherington many hours earlier, swore that he'd sighted a ship, and it was Hetherington's turn to be scornful and to talk about throwing their hand in. 'Calm down,' said Anderson. 'Remember what you said to me.' Hetherington too had a family.

Finally they agreed that once darkness enveloped them they would simply slide off the raft. The German woman was forgotten. Then, in the dying light, they heard a hooter. Simms and Fletcher had found them, near the end of their final sweep.

To the merchant seamen it seemed that the warship must run them down; its bows were rearing above them. But Simms brought his ship smartly alongside. 'Get the woman first,' shouted Hetherington. But while the *Hurricane* crew were trying to do so, the bow wave of the ship broke over the raft and swept the unconscious woman into the sea.

Diving from the deck of the destroyer, Lieutenant George Dudley Pound, son of the Chief of Naval Staff, leapt to her aid, accompanied by an able seaman, and between them they succeeded in securing a bowline around her. Artificial respiration eventually revived her, leading to the paradox that her thanks were spoken in German. She was taken with others to the captain's cabin, and she made a complete recovery.

The chief officer and the purser were the last to be rescued. Anderson was still clutching the safe-custody bag. When they set foot on deck they were greeted by Simms. 'What's your tipple?' Scotsmen both, they answered as one. 'Whisky!'

Imprinted on the minds of the men of HMS *Hurricane* was a montage of ineradicable stills. Simms himself listed some of them. The pallid, sightless faces of children in the lifeboats, their lives beyond recall. The boat with four living and twenty-one dead. The two girls on the bottom of the upturned boat, their frozen fingers almost impossible to unclench. The emotional void of the survivors, most of them too drained even to murmur their thanks, too bludgeoned by tragedy to speak. The tireless efforts of the ship's surgeon and his staff in reviving the exhausted and unconscious. The joy when they were successful, as they were with Johnny Baker, and the inexpressible grief when all three boys rescued with him passed away – first Alan Capel and then, during the evening, Derek Carr and Terence Holmes, in what they had all hoped was a recuperative sleep.

Meanwhile the survivors, having been thawed out in the engine- and boiler-rooms, besides being bathed and fed, were sorted into groups and allocated to the various ward-rooms, cabins and mess-decks, where they were looked after by the men not on duty. The children slept two to a hammock, and although still in weakened condition they managed to laugh. Sailors gave their jerseys and their flannel shirts and used needle and thread to make warm outfits, while navy socks, stockings and scarves were rolled up to make hats.

'The sailors were beyond all praise,' wrote Letitia Quinton. 'They took off their own clothes and dressed us in anything they could find. I wore pyjamas, a dressing-gown and suede shoes. Anthony was dressed as an AB.'

The crew were accustomed to picking up seamen out of the drink, but boats full of women and children, most of them lifeless, brought their war experience to a new pitch of frightfulness. The bowed, silent figure of a German refugee who had already seen more than enough of Nazi brutality needed no caption, and a cold fury gripped them. From now on it would be no quarter asked and none given.

The most moving moment of all came next day, after *Hurricane*, ordered to return to Gourock forthwith, had set course for home. On a bright, sunny morning, with his men lined up on the quarter-deck, Simms read the burial service and three little bodies, draped with a Union Jack, were given a full naval funeral. As the bodies were lowered into the sea and disappeared slowly, the solemnity of the occasion overcame many. Each was paying homage to the eighty-three children lost of the ninety who had set out to cross the Atlantic five days before.

The seven survivors were Beth Cummings, Bess and Louis Walder, Eleanor Wright, Rex Thorne, Jack Keeley and Johnny Baker – three girls and four boys. The last two were the only evacuee children under ten to come through.

Of the privately booked children under sixteen, an infinitely greater proportion, six out of ten, had survived. They were the three Bech children, Tony Quinton, Pat Bulmer (who lost her mother and schoolfriend) and Colin Ryder Richardson. Most had been accommodated in the forepart of the ship, rather than astern, where the torpedo struck, but they had suffered equally during the launching, and in the boats and on rafts, so there seems no obvious reason for the discrepancy. Yet whereas the evacuee children were allocated to boats in groups of fifteen, restricting the care that could be devoted to any one child, the fare-paying children, at two or three to a boat, suffered no such dilution, and indeed several adults took these children into their personal care.

Almost as harrowing as the losses was the anguish of survivors, as they recovered their strength, in scouring the ship for missing relatives and friends. Escort Lilian Towns was deputed to sit with Margaret Hodgson, who threatened to kill herself when her husband's absence from the rescue list was confirmed. Rex Thorne asked in vain for his sister Marion – 'Mary for Short' – and Jack Keeley for the six-year-old Joyce. Pat Bulmer mourned her mother and schoolfriend, the Choat family a husband and father, Monika Lanyi her husband. Yet there were poignant reunions. Ten-year-old Louis Walder shouted with delight when he recognized his sister's dressing-gown hanging up to dry in the boiler-room; among the evacuee children they were the only pair from one family to survive.

How fortunate they were can be gauged from the many whole families of children swept completely away. All five of the Grimmonds, a tragedy surely without parallel;

three brothers Pugh from Liverpool; three Beasley girls – Vera, Phyllis and Edna – from Winchmore Hill, London; three Moss sisters, from Newport; the two flaxen-haired Spencer children; Rosemary and John Spencer-Davies; the two boys in quarantine, Alan Capel and Peter Short, and their respective brothers, Derek and Billy. Also missing were the two children who had survived the *Volendam* sinking and been forced by domestic circumstances to travel again, Patricia Allen and Michael Brooker. The list of personal tragedies was endless, among children and grown-ups alike.

Equally poignant, and totally mystifying, was the complete disappearance of Boat 12. *Hurricane*'s limits of search had deliberately erred on the generous side, the approach had been made upwind, and it seemed inconceivable that a fully loaded lifeboat, as this one was known to have been, could have escaped their notice. Some thought it had been overloaded: there were more than forty people in it, the majority of them Lascars, when it was last seen. Yet as one of the only two unflooded boats at that time, with ample freeboard, it had been the envy of other boats. Even the capsized boats had remained buoyant and had still been visible, but Ronnie Cooper's boat, with a complement that included two escorts – Mary Cornish and Father O'Sullivan – and six boys, had vanished. Yet when the state of the other boats was examined, the disappearance of one boat seemed less remarkable. Some freak of the elements must have overwhelmed it.

One of the *Marina*'s two boats was also missing, but it had been under the command of the ship's master, Captain R. T. Paine. Paine, with a crew of sixteen merchant seamen, was known to have hoisted sail and set course for Ireland early on the morning after the sinking

– something quite beyond the scope of any of the *Benares* boats – which explained why they were not seen by *Hurricane*.

When Johnny Baker recovered he escaped from his escorts and sought out the captain. 'Have you seen my brother?' he piped. 'When you speak to me,' replied Simms with a twinkle, 'you address me as Captain.' The seven-year-old was quite unabashed. 'Captain – have you seen my brother?' Sadly, no one had.

The tragedy affected no one more deeply than Hugh Crofton Simms, who from that moment dedicated his life to an unspoken resolve for retributive justice. He sensed, too, from the strangely subdued atmosphere that suffused the ship on the way back to Gourock and after, that his crew felt the same. 'Pity the poor Hun who meets *Hurricane*,' he wrote.

All seven evacuee children were cured of their wander-lust, at least for the moment, and longed for reunion with loved ones. 'We're not going to Canada, are we?' they asked. 'Are we going home?' 'Yes,' they were told, 'we're going home.'

It was only human nature, Simms supposed, that the survivors should revert to type, though he was disillusioned with the way they 'classed up', as he called it, in what he was proud to describe as a classless ship, separating into status groups almost at once. Comradeship in the lifeboats, where it had existed, was quickly forgotten. There was evidence, too, of racial animosity and prejudice, manifested in bitter recriminations between European and Asian, which reached a hysterical pitch on the night of the rescue.

Steaming at 20 knots all the way back, *Hurricane*

entered the North Channel at 04.00 on Friday, 20 September and the survivors were landed at Greenock at 11.00, to be met by Geoffrey Shakespeare himself. News of the sinking had been censored, and was not to be released until relatives were told. But a signal sent by Simms to C.-in-C. Western Approaches at 22.30 on 18 September, partly culled from the appalling stories heard from survivors, had caused such perturbation to the Admiralty, the Ministry of Shipping and to Shakespeare himself that already the projected sailing of the second Lascar-crewed Ellerman ship, *City of Simla*, carrying thirty Scottish children to South Africa, had been postponed so that the children could be disembarked. This is what was transmitted:

18 women and 15 children, 48 men, 36 Lascars saved from SS *Marina* and *City of Benares*. One boat missing *Marina* under sail. There are no other survivors alive from *City of Benares*, all boats from *City of Benares* were rushed by Lascars and capsized. Investigation required on arrival. Two further children died on board *Hurricane*. Commodore of convoy and captain missing. Most women and children saved are without husbands, parents or money. Please inform High Commissioner, Canada, French Aviation Officer, Secret Mission, has been saved. HURRICANE 2230/18.

In passing this message to the Admiralty, with its implications of a complete breakdown in crew discipline on the *Benares*, causing the boats to capsize, Admiral Sir Martin Nasmith, C.-in-C. Western Approaches, thought fit to add: '*Request Ministry of Shipping be asked to carry out necessary investigation.*'

7

'This Deed will Shock the World'

The buff-coloured envelope that dropped on the doormat of 59 homes on the morning of Friday 20 September in four corners of Britain – in Sunderland, in Liverpool, in Cardiff and Newport, and in London and the South – contained a message of heartrending woe. The letter inside got straight to the point; this is what parents were faced with when they slit open the envelope, still hoping against hope – for most of them had had prior warning from social workers – and drew out the letter.

I am very distressed to inform you that in spite of all the precautions taken the ship carrying your child/children to Canada was torpedoed on Tuesday night September 17th. I am afraid your child/children is/are not among those reported as rescued and I am informed that there is no chance of there being any further lists of survivors from the torpedoed vessel.

Parents did not need to read further, and indeed many of them were rendered incapable of doing so. The screams of one bereaved mother brought out a whole street in sympathy, and an eye-witness writes: 'It was like a scene from a pit disaster.' A school in Wembley assembled after an 'All Clear' to learn that seven recent pupils had been lost: one of them was Rex Thorne's sister Marion. The Board felt the need to ease parents' remorse by justifying their decision, for all its tragic consequences, and they also felt the need for self-justification. Thus the second paragraph of the letter, after offering the Board's very deep sympathy, included the following:

Like so many other parents you were anxious to send your children overseas to one of the Dominions to enjoy a happier and safer life. You courageously took this decision in the interest of the children . . . Hitherto there have been no casualties among the thousands of children sent overseas; unhappily the course of the war has shown that neither by land nor sea can there be complete safety . . .

The sincerity of the Board's sympathy is not in question. But they obviously recognized at this early stage that they might come under attack.

On Sunday, 22 September, by which time all parents had been informed, a statement was issued and facilities were granted to the Press, newsreels and radio for interviewing, photographing and filming survivors. Next morning, Monday the 23rd, the sinking was front-page news in the world Press. The text of the statement issued began:

The Children's Overseas Reception Board announces with regret that a ship conveying 90 children and 9 escorts [there were 10] to Canada under its scheme of evacuation from vulnerable areas to the overseas dominions has been torpedoed and sunk. It is feared that 83 of the children and 7 of the escorts have been lost . . .

As with the evacuee ship which was torpedoed late in August on a similar voyage, when the whole company of 320 [there were 321] children were saved unharmed, the precautions taken by the Board were on the scale which made it possible to transport overseas and place in homes nearly 3,000 children [it was actually well short of 3,000] without, hitherto, a single casualty.

Again it was natural that the Board should feel on the defensive, as their next paragraph confirmed. 'The tragic circumstances defeated all precautions . . . There was a heavy sea which swamped boats and defeated gallant efforts at rescue.' Nothing was said of the departure of the escort, or of the failure of the convoy to disperse, or of the report of Lascar seamen rushing the boats. But the first of these factors, at least, was implicit in the accounts that followed.

The first depositions taken from European crew members suggested that all allegations passed on in the *Hurricane* signal about the Lascars had been based on the evidence of passengers suffering at the time from a state of hysteria. However, it was realized that crew members, and especially the ship's officers, might not be impartial witnesses, since panic or incompetence in any part of the crew would reflect on them. Further depositions, from crew members and passengers, were awaited to help with the full investigation that was being called for by both the Admiralty and the Ministry of Shipping.

Meanwhile Geoffrey Shakespeare issued his own personal statement. 'I am full of horror and indignation that any German submarine captain could be found to torpedo a ship over 600 miles from land in a tempestuous sea. The conditions were such that there was little chance for passengers, whether adults or children, to survive. This deed will shock the world . . .'

Almost without exception, world opinion endorsed Shakespeare's reaction of righteous indignation, and the sinking brought widespread opprobrium for Nazi Germany. 'I am sure there will be no division of opinion in this country,' wrote Cordell Hull, the United States Secretary of State, 'that this was a most dastardly act.' One US Congressman called Hitler 'The Mad Butcher'. In Canada the minister directing the work of receiving and placing the evacuees called it 'just another demonstration of Nazi frightfulness'. R. G. Menzies, the Australian Prime Minister, forecast that 'this latest exhibition of savagery by the Nazis' would steel the British people to 'defeat the dark spirit for which the Nazi regime stands'. And from the Australian Consolidated Press: 'This brutal sinking will shock and horrify the whole civilized world.'

British newspapers, naturally enough, were in the vanguard of the vituperation. 'Murder at Sea', 'Revolting Tragedy', 'Nazi Inhumanity', 'Criminal Disaster', 'Bestial Crime' – these were among the more extravagant expressions of censure. They would have made little impression on the Nazis by themselves, but a Gallup Poll taken in America in the wake of the incident showed that Americans were now far more ready than before to risk their neutrality to help Britain.

Most of these strictures were based on a naïve belief in Nazi omniscience, an illusion which credited the enemy with a knowledge of Allied shipping movements and cargoes carried which it did not possess. Bleichrodt had shadowed the convoy for many hours and had had plenty of time to pick out the fruitiest target, which in this case was easily identifiable as a sizeable modern passenger liner, but it wasn't until he heard the SOS that he knew which ship he had hit, and even then he did not know what she carried. Even if he had, his orders, however much they offended against international law, would have obliged him to attack and destroy such valuable Allied tonnage. To what extent, if any, could Bleichrodt be held responsible? The *City of Benares* had every appearance of being an important vessel to the British, as indeed she was, and she was leading a formation of nineteen merchant ships. In addition she was armed, however inadequately. It was on this weakness in the British position that the Nazi propaganda machine, with a typical mixture of truth, lies and innuendo, concentrated when the impact on American public opinion became clear.

As early as Saturday, 21 September, before the news of the sinking was released by the British, a Berlin communiqué boasted of the successes of one Kapitänleutnant Bleichrodt, who was said to have sunk on his latest cruise nine steamers totalling 51,862 tons, one of the outstanding U-boat cruises of the war. This figure included the *City of Benares*, although no names were mentioned. But when the loss was announced and its implications became clear, Goebbels entered the argument.

At first he issued an official denial: no passenger vessel identifiable as such had been torpedoed by any German U-boat or plane, either within or outside the blockade zone announced on 18 August. Further, not so much as a freighter had been torpedoed outside this zone unless it was clearly armed. Naval circles protested that no U-boat or plane had been operating as far as 600 miles out from the English coast. The story of the sinking of a British refugee ship was a brazen lie, a tearjerker, a Churchillian trick to get the United States into the war on the British side. (Goebbels had made precisely the same accusation when the *Athenia* was sunk on the first day of the war.) If it proved that the ship had really been sunk, it could have been a mine of British origin that did it. But the whole story had been fabricated to furnish a talking-point for a surprise broadcast made by King George VI on the evening of the news release.

A reference to the sinking was indeed made in the King's broadcast on the evening of 23 September, although the speech was originally prepared as a review of the first year of the war; the section on the *City of Benares* was clearly an insertion. 'And here,' said the King, 'I would like to tell the sorrowing parents how deeply we grieve for them over the loss of their children in the ship torpedoed without warning in mid-Atlantic.

Surely the world could have no clearer proof of the wickedness against which we fight than this foul deed.' The last sentence, as Goebbels no doubt realized, was purposely aimed at neutral opinion. And as corroborative details of the incident were splashed on front pages all over the free world, with pictures of survivors, Goebbels changed his tune.

The pretence of German innocence was only casually maintained. Germany did not sink the *City of Benares* – but if they did they were justified in doing so. The ship had been taken over by the Admiralty and converted into an armed merchant cruiser, which justified its sinking by all the rules of warfare. (Britain had certainly turned passenger liners into armed merchant cruisers, but the *City of Benares* was not one of them.) In a plausible blend of mocking insinuation and specious half-truth that was not without humour, Goebbels suggested that 'the device of putting children in auxiliary cruisers and calling them children's export ships might be extended to munitions factories; through the presence of a few children they could acquire the status of orphanages'. The British government alone was responsible, for it was they who sent the children to their doom in the face of repeated German warnings not to send children into the danger zone (in fact the warnings were addressed to the Americans, when they asked for safe conduct for their ships; but a degree of government responsibility was undeniable). Finally, he looked for a scapegoat, though he did not hunt very far. 'If the ship was really torpedoed with the loss of eighty-three children, then the murderer's name is Churchill. Nothing is sacred to this monster.'

It was inevitable that Churchill should be Goebbels' Aunt Sally. But as we have seen, Churchill had no hand in the evacuation scheme and deprecated it from the first.

If anyone was guilty of risking the children's necks for a principle it wasn't Churchill.

Criticism of the CORB scheme was almost non-existent in Britain, and leading articles vied with each other to urge that this admittedly tragic setback should be kept in proportion. 'Far more than these eighty-three drowned children have been murdered in the last ten days by the same enemy,' said the *News Chronicle*, 'and they have been murdered here in London. We should remember also that more than 3,000 British children have already crossed the oceans of the world and are beyond the reach of German malice.' 'Take a look at the morgues,' was another comment. 'That's why we're sending them away.' It was a recurring theme that the incident must on no account be allowed to slow up the speed of overseas evacuation. 'Heartrending though this criminal disaster is,' said *The Times*, 'it does not reflect on the policy of sending children to safety overseas.'

One of the few discordant notes came from the *Daily Mail*, which questioned whether the government was satisfied with the arrangements that had been made for the children's safety. No one else seems to have picked up the point that at the time of the sinking the naval escort had left, but the *Mail* asked specifically 'whether the ships were convoyed far enough out to sea'. As for the argument in mitigation that 3,000 children had been transported overseas up to this point without a single casualty, they dismissed this as 'an insufficient answer'. 'Still more must be done,' insisted the *Mail*, 'to prevent a repetition of this intolerable tragedy.' Here was a clear indication that public disquiet might stimulate demands for a full and open enquiry.

The *Glasgow Herald* took such an enquiry for granted. 'The Nazi methods of warfare being what we know them to be, no precautions can be too elaborate to ensure that the risk of a mishap, especially to children for whom the government have in a sense accepted responsibility, is reduced to a minimum . . . It is to be hoped that the investigation will lead to a thorough revision of the precautions and safeguards employed.'

In the country as a whole the reaction remained one of outrage, accompanied by intemperate demands for revenge. There were appeals from religious leaders not to sink to the enemy's level whatever the provocation, but these were far outnumbered by demands that kid-glove methods be finally discarded. The Nazis, it was argued, could only be defeated by policies of equal ruthlessness.

Churchill, visiting the bombed areas of South London on the day after the *Benares* sinking was revealed, was asked: 'Are we going to make any reprisals?' He avoided this one at first, but when pressed on the point he said, 'Yes – all in good time.' Four days later, in a minute for the Chiefs of Staff Committee, he wrote: 'The possibility of our having to retaliate on the German civil population must be studied, and on the largest scale possible. We should never begin, but must be able to reply.' The trouble with international law in wartime, as the bombed-out were quick to perceive, was that there was no means of enforcing it except by reprisals.

The reaction of the bereaved showed a commendable absence of vindictiveness or recrimination, though to begin with their voices were doubtless muted by grief and remorse. It was axiomatic that they had been doing what they thought best for their children, they took Nazi ruthlessness for granted, and they were not unaware of the risks. But a feeling that they had gambled with their children's lives and lost was inevitable, and this was what Geoffrey Shakespeare, in addition to defending the

CORB scheme, had been at pains to assuage. That there might be a backlash was not unforeseen.

One man who gave vent to his feelings, not surprisingly, was Eddie Grimmond, father of the redoubtable Gussie, lost together with Violet, Connie, Eddie junior, and the incorrigible Lenny, who walked about on the liner in those first few days 'as though nothing had happened'. 'This is not war,' said Grimmond senior, 'this is cold-blooded murder.' His grief and resentment led him to abandon his job as a council labourer and seek to rejoin his First World War regiment, the King's Royal Rifle Corps. 'I'm going to join up and try to get a front-line job,' he said. 'My only wish is to find some way to get back at the Nazis.' He mourned Gussie above all, and never got over his loss.

In Wembley, which had also suffered extensively from the bombing – so much so that the King and Queen paid a visit to demolished areas later that week – Rex Thorne's father was typically defiant. 'If Rex is able to go to Canada and wants to go again I shan't stop him. I know there would have been a fine future for my children in Canada.' Of 'Mary for Short' he said: 'Marion was a fine girl and so eager to go.' But he added: 'Her mother has taken the shock badly.' Rex was the sole survivor of a party of thirteen from Wembley, just as Eleanor Wright was of the eleven from Sunderland and Beth Cummings of the twelve from Liverpool. Of the twelve Welsh children, not one returned.

In all the provincial areas concerned, and locally in and around London, obituary notices were published, school assemblies stood for one minute's silence and memorial services were held. The losses were exceptionally severe among the children and their escorts, as the figures showed.

	Total	Lost	Percentage
European Crew	43	25	58
Asian Crew	166	133	80
Convoy Staff	6	3	50
Passengers (Fare-paying)	91	52	57
CORB Escorts	10	8	80
CORB Children	90	83	92
	406	304	

The area of the disaster had been so systematically quartered by *Hurricane* that although Simms was haunted by the fear that he might have missed someone in the water during his six-hour search, no straggler could have lasted more than another few hours, and with a five-day interval between the rescue of survivors by *Hurricane* and the news announcement, during which nothing of interest was reported by any other vessel, government sources were able to state categorically that there was no hope of any other survivors. Hope was held out, however, for the sixteen merchant seamen in the second *Marina* lifeboat, under Captain Paine. When last seen they had hoisted sail, they had oars on board, with plenty of oarsmen, and Captain Paine's intention of making for land if all else failed was known in the other *Marina* boat.

Paine hoped to make land in a week, and he put his men on a daily ration of three dry biscuits and a dipper of water each. After six days the water gave out and the men were too weak to eat the dry biscuit, but on the eighth day Tory Island Light was sighted, north of Bloody Foreland, Donegal, and a coaster took the sixteen exhausted men on board and towed their boat to Londonderry. Ten of the sixteen, including Captain Paine, were taken to hospital.

This copybook open-boat voyage, for which Paine highly commended his crew, seemed to hold no significance for those who were mourning relatives and friends lost with the *City of Benares*. But in fact Ronnie Cooper's boat, Boat 12, with forty-six people on board, including six children, was still afloat.

How had it evaded the exhaustive box search made by HMS *Hurricane*? Who else was on board? And where were they now?

8

Back from the Dead

The last lee-side boat to be launched had been Boat 12, and it was also the farthest astern; thus by the time it was lowered to the water the way was off the ship and the warring currents alongside the hull which had swamped other boats had subsided. Twenty-two-year-old Fourth Officer Ronnie Cooper was thus able to get clear and lay off in good order by use of the Fleming gear until the *Benares* sank, thus escaping the tidal-bore effect of the sinking as well.

Many of the first boats to be launched were lowered in a hurry, and more than one of the forward boats was lowered straight to the water without stopping at an intervening deck. With the ship already listing and down by the stern, giving every appearance of sinking within minutes, and with the fear of a possible second torpedo adding to the urgency, haste was natural. Ronnie Cooper, at the stern on the lee side, was in a better position than those forward to assess how imminent sinking was, and he took his time.

Only five feet six inches tall, chunkily built, and shy to the point of taciturnity, Cooper was an unflappable Taysider; he came from a seafaring family (his father and mother had both been to sea and he had four seafaring brothers), and he walked with a roll. If some were impatient of his calm deliberation on deck they were glad of it now, especially those who, in the next half-hour, he was able to reach and pick out of the water or off rafts. Among these were Cadet Doug Critchley, naval signaller

Johnny Mayhew, naval gunner Harry Peard and ten Lascars, to add to the twenty-two Lascars already in the boat. Others who had embarked earlier were assistant steward George Purvis, escorts Father O'Sullivan and Mary Cornish, and the six boys who had escaped with Father O'Sullivan from the blocked cabins. They were: Derek Capel, twelve, of Hanworth, Middlesex, older brother of the unfortunate Alan; Billy Short, nine, of Sunderland, who was also missing a quarantined younger brother; Kenneth Sparks, thirteen, from Wembley, oldest of the six; and three eleven-year-olds – Howard Claytor from Kenton, Middlesex, Paul Shearing from Bourne-mouth, and Freddie Steels from Eastleigh, Southampton. All these boys, seeking adventure, had persuaded their parents to let them go to Canada under the government scheme.

O'Sullivan was only thirty-two, but seasickness and a chill had so sapped his strength that the direction into this boat by Joe Hetherington of Mary Cornish looked like proving a happy chance.

There was only one fare-paying passenger on board, and this was the Polish shipping executive Bohdan Nagorski, still wearing the apparel – black overcoat, Homburg hat, kid gloves – which had contrasted so oddly with the lightly clad Lascars.

The boat was no less affected by the rough seas and heavy swell than most others, but although its occupants were continually drenched, having started off with a dry boat they were able to keep pace with the influx of water by baling. When the moon appeared from behind a cloud it revealed in dramatic three-dimensional form the mountainous seascape that almost engulfed them, deep valleys alternating with apparently snow-capped peaks, so that one moment they were perched on precipitous crests before toppling next moment into seemingly fathomless troughs. Cooper doubted if they could stand much of this, and when he saw a light which he took to be from a rescue ship he set his crew to the Fleming gear and tried to steer towards it. They made little progress, but he got close enough to find out that it was only another lifeboat. Which one was it? He had seen what had happened to the other lee-side boats during launching, and he couldn't place this one.

'What ship are you?' asked a voice.

'The *City of Benares*. And you?'

'*Marina.*'

So that was it. He knew another ship in the convoy had been hit. This was the second of the *Marina*'s boats, the one with Captain Paine in command. Seeing no sign of other boats, Cooper elected to keep company with this one. Paine had decided to remain in the vicinity of the sinking until daybreak in the hope of a rescue craft appearing by then, and this suited Cooper. Both boats were drifting in an easterly direction before the strong south-westerly, and both were keeping sea and swell astern. The other boats must be similarly affected, so they would be visible in the morning. Meanwhile, as they were continually drenched and hailstones and wind-chill aggravated their discomfort, Cooper was glad to have another boat in sight. That would make them easier to find when rescue came, as he fully expected, at dawn.

One man who felt uneasy at the loss of contact with the other *Benares* boats, however, was Nagorski. He felt they ought to be doing what they could to follow up behind the convoy; surely one of the other ships would stop to pick up survivors. This view, as Cooper knew, was not only impractical but mistaken. Progress to the west was out of the question, and no ship in the convoy would stop. But

Paine and Cooper were mistaken, too, in imagining that the *Benares* boats would be drifting with them. Because their boats were unflooded, they retained much more freeboard than the other *Benares* boats. With a much greater surface area exposed to the wind, they were being driven along more rapidly by it. This was why, when daylight came – grey, sullen and stormy – no other boats were in sight.

There was no sign of any rescue craft either, and Captain Paine decided he must take the initiative. The Irish coast was some 650 miles distant, but rather than wait about for rescue that might never come he resolved to make an attempt to reach it. He estimated that if wind and weather remained westerly he could make it in about a week. Strict rationing would be necessary, so the sooner he started the better. At 08.30 he parted company from the *Benares* boat and set sail.

Cooper's problems were fundamentally different. Whereas Paine had a skilled, compact and disciplined crew, Cooper had an overcrowded boat with a mixed complement that included thirty-two Lascars (many of them Goanese stewards who were not strictly seamen at all), a woman and six children. He had only a handful of men whose abilities might be of practical use in sailing and navigating an open boat. Although he had one of the biggest of the *Benares* boats – it was thirty feet long – propinquity was already causing cramp and ill-temper. It could well take them much more than a week to reach land, yet if they had really been left behind by the rescue ship that was the challenge he seemed likely to face.

As a preliminary, Cooper reorganized the seating. He moved passengers, escorts and children into the bows, where Purvis and Mayhew rigged a canvas hood to give them some protection. Two handles of the Fleming gear

were removed to make more room. The Lascars were
distributed in the middle of the boat, sitting on the thwarts
or the gunwales or lying down in the bottom, with the
European crew in the stern. Cooper then checked the
amount of food and water on board and formulated a
rationing plan, detailing George Purvis – 'Georgy Porgy',
as he came to be known – to dole out the agreed quantities
twice daily.

Water was the commodity that governed their chances
of survival, and Cooper found he had nearly 10.5 gallons
on board, which worked out at 1.4 quarts per person. He
would have to restrict the water issue to two 'dippers' –
less than a quarter of a pint per dipper – per day. He
could hardly issue less, he felt, but dare not give more.
Food was less restricted, though it consisted almost exclusively of tinned corned beef, sardines and salmon, tins of
condensed milk and the inevitable ship's biscuits.

Another pressing need that morning was to make some
sort of sanitary arrangements. Privacy was impossible,
and a bucket and a baler were passed round as occasion
demanded. But between times both bucket and baler
were needed to keep the boat reasonably dry, and soon
the bucket was reserved exclusively for 'Auntie Mary'.
When it was called for the question would be asked: 'Who
wants it?' Entering into the game, the Lascars would
reply: 'The memsahib!' And the bucket would be passed
forward.

It was no good being prudish in these circumstances,
and when Mary Cornish heard they were looking for some
sort of flag to flutter from the mast-top to improve their
chances of being seen she donated her petticoat, to the
delight of the boys. Mayhew shinned up the mast and tied
this on, together with a towel.

Gale and swell were so vicious that morning, however,

that Cooper decided not to follow Captain Paine's example as yet. He had not quite given up hope of rescue, and with his load he might easily broach to in heavy seas and capsize. Instead, he got the Fleming gear going again, set an easterly course, and organized his European crew into watches. Progress would not be dramatic, and a search would still find them.

Working the levers that ran fore and aft inside the boat, now reduced to four either side, caused much disturbance and annoyance to those seated near them, many of them Lascars, but at least they provided some exercise, and even the boys did their share. Nagorski, however, was again silently critical and he offered no help with the levers. Their chances of reaching land with the means at their disposal seemed to him infinitesimal. They should stay where they were.

For Cooper, too, the prospect of covering 650 miles in these conditions was more than daunting; he knew it was the most forlorn of hopes. It would be triumph enough even for Captain Paine if he made it, with all his advantages. Yet as the day advanced he became resigned to the conclusion that the searchers had missed them, and that to wait until shortage of water ruled out the only alternative was unacceptable. They must have a go, and they would have the same chance of being picked up, even perhaps a better one, if they tried to reach land.

Cooper had been lucky in the men he had picked out of the sea. In Doug Critchley he was greatly encouraged to find he had an experienced amateur yachtsman; he doubted if he could have attempted such a voyage without him. Purvis combined firmness and efficiency over the rations with unfailing good temper. Mayhew had gained his sea legs on destroyers. And if it took him rather longer to appreciate the abrasive, rough-diamond willingness of

Peard, he came to rate him, for cheerfulness and tirelessness, as second to none.

He was also extremely fortunate in having aboard a Lascar general servant named Ramjam, whose demeanour while assisting passengers into the boats had impressed him and steadied his fellows and whose influence on his compatriots now promised to be crucial. At present the Lascars were docile, but Cooper did not forget that they outnumbered the European crew members by more than six to one and could well take control of the boat if they were minded to do so.

Gradually they established a routine. Purvis doled out the rations at midday and tea-time, Father O'Sullivan said grace and led them in prayers, and at night, and sometimes after the midday meal, Mary Cornish told the boys a story. Her main character was an amalgam of Bulldog Drummond and Richard Hannay, and she thrilled the boys with his lone exploits against villains and spies and Nazis and his survivals against odds, weaving in every narrative trick she could think of and always ending on a cliffhanger of suspense which left the boys in delicious expectation of the next instalment. They hardly wanted to be rescued until the denouement was revealed. More serious matters intruded next morning, however, when the weather moderated and Cooper, ignoring the brooding scepticism of Nagorski, had the sails hoisted and set course for Ireland.

Militating against cooperation and crew spirit, and even against communication, was the congestion. Mixing was minimal and the passengers in the bows were isolated from the crew in the stern, as remote and inaccessible to each other as in a rush-hour tube train, with the barrier of the Lascars in between. The one person small and nimble enough to get around the boat – and who didn't mind over-much whom he inconvenienced – was Harry Peard, who somehow contrived to be in several places at once.

Peard's sorties and sallies were not universally popular, and to some he was not far short of a pest. But he knew how to manage the Lascars, and to the boys especially he was a continual source of diversion and humour. Accustomed to his daily dip, when the water was calm he swam round the boat, floundering deliberately to scare the boys and make them laugh. His idea was to show them there was nothing in their environment to be afraid of. 'Why are you going swimming, mister?' asked one of the boys. Peard had his answer ready. 'To keep in practice, in case we get torpedoed again.' The notion of a thirty-foot lifeboat being torpedoed spread laughter right through the boat.

Peard's method of jollying people out of the doldrums was to stimulate them, often by being gratuitously offensive, so that they had to react. Even the escorts didn't escape; he thought them too genteel and sedate. There were too many prayers, he said, and they cosseted the children too much. With three children of his own, he tended to deride the fuss that was made of these boys by the escorts. A celibate priest, and a spinster – what could they know about kids, having none of their own? He spared them none of these sentiments, his fruitier observations were not all delivered out of earshot, and he kept everyone on their toes. Cooper seldom restrained him – he was good for morale.

Even Nagorski did not escape. Peard chided him for his aloofness, and for spending much of his time drying out his bank roll. Nagorski responded by giving him a fiver. 'What's the use of that here?' Peard muttered to himself. 'I see no shops.' But he pocketed the money. Later, when

Nagorski heard the boys bemoaning their lost pocket-money – it had been held for them by one of the missing escorts – he promised to make it up to them when they were rescued.

The boys took turns to squeeze two at a time into a cubby-hole in the bows, where they were completely protected under the tarpaulin. But they suffered severely from cramps, and Mary Cornish and others were continually massaging their limbs and their feet. Constipation was chronic, but they continued to pass water freely. They were beginning to dehydrate; the deprivation they felt was of liquid, not food.

Of the boys, Paul Shearing was suffering most, with a form of trench-feet caused by immersion, but they all suffered from it in varying degree. For all the baling they did, they could never rid themselves of a few inches of water in the bottom of the boat. Paul was one of two Bournemouth children – the other was a girl, Jean Forster – who were the last to be selected for the voyage; the girl had been one of a group tipped out of a lifeboat, and she hadn't survived.

Paul had used a good deal of subterfuge to get into the scheme in the first place; his parents had agreed to his elder brother going, but not Paul. He had collected the application forms himself, and got his sister to talk his mother into it. At the last moment his brother, more deeply involved in school activities, had elected not to go, but this hadn't discouraged Paul. When the *Volendam* sank and his trip was postponed he was in tears; now, in the lifeboat, he knew he could blame no one but himself. At least he didn't have a brother to worry about, as did Derek and Billy.

On Friday afternoon, 20 September, the day the survivors from the other boats were landed at Greenock, the westerly wind increased to gale force, with blustery rain squalls and mountain-range seas. Cooper and Critchley, working together, were forced to take down the sails and ride to a sea anchor, which they made fast to the after end of the boat, their object of riding astern to the sea being to keep the children and others up front as dry as they could. It was an unceasing struggle to keep stern up to the waves, and as the seas were often coming at them from two directions at once they had to try to bisect them, avoiding the worst of each. Several times when Critchley was at the tiller a wave crashed almost simultaneously over either shoulder and he had to call for vigorous baling. One moment they were sitting under a precipice that seemed about to avalanche, next came a moment of vertigo as they were buoyed to the summit. Throughout the day they were in danger of being overwhelmed.

For the boys, memories of the thrills of the fairground were totally eclipsed. There was no roller-coaster to compare with an open boat in an Atlantic storm, and they endured it with a mixture of exhilaration and terror. As night fell the boat seemed certain to overturn, and the close proximity of bodies and the boat's protrusions left them battered and bruised. Yet continuous baling restricted the flooding, and somehow the boat was still stable at dawn.

Father O'Sullivan had little chance to recover his normally robust health in these conditions, and he was often prostrate with seasickness, but his belief in the power of prayer, and the regular prayers he offered, sustained him and, he hoped, comforted the boys. He made them promise that if rescue came they would not forget a prayer of thanksgiving. But such an outcome looked more remote each day. It was the music teacher who assumed the main task of keeping the boys occupied, forcing a grudging respect from Peard. Her story-telling became reminiscent of the *Arabian Nights*, except that it was the lives of the boys she was seeking to preserve, not simply her own.

As a relief from stories, guessing games, quizzes and prayers, which he regarded as too puritanical a diet for the boys, Peard taught them Cockney songs, the earthier the better, and he got them to join in, after suitable coaching, with such music-hall favourites as 'Any Old Iron' and 'My Old Man said Follow the Van'. The boys could take liberties with Peard that they couldn't take with their escorts, and this gave them a friend on their own level. 'What's his name?' he heard them ask. 'Is it Harry? There – see that? He looked up! It's Harry all right!' His impudent clowning was just what they needed to cheer them up and set them talking among themselves.

One of his keenest admirers was Nagorski, who by this time approved wholeheartedly of the crew in the lifeboat, though he was critical of the provisioning. Water was the vital ingredient and there was not enough of it, not for a voyage of 600-odd miles. Since the human body could exist for long periods on water alone, why hadn't more been provided? They couldn't even eat the dry rations without water. The biscuits were so unyielding that they began to use them as plates to balance their sardines and bully beef on, rather than as food. Condensed milk only made them more than ever thirsty for water.

Nagorski was also critical of the shortage of blankets. He was well covered himself, but both children and Lascars were pitifully clad. The Lascars found and appropriated what few blankets there were, but they gave one to the children and during the storm were persuaded to give up another, so that the children could wrap themselves three to a blanket. Father O'Sullivan gave them full marks for this, as he could see how severely they were suffering. Their background and diet ill-prepared them for such an ordeal, and there were times when their restless murmurings – they chattered incessantly – seemed about to reach flash-point. Their help with the Fleming gear was no more than sporadic. But they were scared, disheartened and lethargic rather than mutinous, and on the whole Ramjam managed them well. One of his tasks was to stop the younger ones drinking sea water.

Early on the fourth day, Saturday, the storm abated and they set sail again on their easterly course. They made fair progress, but again thirst caused friction, the Lascars suspecting that they weren't getting their share. In any case, they said, they wanted more. Fortunately Purvis was so efficient and methodical in distributing the rations that he was able to convince them, with the help of Ramjam and some bullying humour from Peard, that they were getting the maximum that the slender supplies allowed.

That afternoon O'Sullivan, recovered from his seasickness, suddenly pointed to a school of whales, a thrilling sight as they cavorted near the boat. But the possibility that they might overturn the boat scared the Lascars, and for once they showed great animation, operating the hand-levers frantically to get away. O'Sullivan always sought to interest the boys in the wonders of nature, and he pointed out fishes that flashed like fire at night, and magnificent sunsets. But there were beginning to be hallucinations too.

On Sunday Purvis promised them all a special treat: it came at midday in the shape of a segment each of canned peach. Crisp and cool, it eased and lubricated their parched throats voluptuously. After the meal, a gulp of peach juice helped to eke out the water.

They were battling along steadily on Sunday afternoon, their fifth day in the boat, when they sighted a ship. It seemed to be heading straight for them, and in great excitement they fired off their only two rockets. It looked like a small cargo vessel, four or five miles distant, but visibility was good and they were sure they'd be seen. For some minutes the ship held its course, and while Mayhew signalled SOS repeatedly with the semaphore flags the others began to gather up their belongings and get ready to leave. Then to their chagrin the ship appeared to change course, not towards them but away. They shouted and waved, but the ship steamed remorselessly on, until its silhouette receded and dimmed. Tantalized almost beyond enduring, they argued among themselves as they searched for a reason. Could the ship have been on a zig-zag course to avoid U-boats, and somehow missed seeing them on the leg nearest to them? Were they suspected of being a decoy? Or was it an enemy ship? Cooper thought they simply hadn't been seen: they were no more than a tiny speck, intermittently visible in a choppy sea.

Whatever the answer, they were not only dejected but mortified. They had expended their rockets in vain.[1]

Peard was as disrespectful to his navigators as he was to everyone else, audibly doubting their ability, but he supported them now, pulling his shipmates up off the floor. 'What's the matter? Nothing to be downhearted

---

[1] The ship may have been HMS *Ascania*, an old Cunarder converted in wartime to an armed merchant cruiser. She was returning to her base in Halifax, Nova Scotia after handing over to a local escort off the Irish coast when one of her look-outs reported seeing a ship's lifeboat 'with what looked like children aboard', but nothing more was seen and he was told he must have imagined it. *Ascania* steamed on for Halifax.

about. We must be in the shipping lanes. There'll be another one along in a minute!' But there wasn't.

Cooper felt obliged to reduce the water ration. How long could they last? Ten days? Perhaps a fortnight for some of them? There would be deaths in the boat before then. To counteract this latest low point in their fortunes, Father O'Sullivan, the only Roman Catholic in the boat apart from the Goanese, got the boys to recite the Hail Mary after him sentence by sentence. He did not know that his own mother, back at his home in Herne Bay, was having nightly visions of him clinging to a raft, that his death had been reported, that a Requiem Mass was being celebrated that evening in his memory, and that his obituary notice had been prepared, to appear in the next issue of the magazine *Universe*.

By that Sunday evening the next of kin of all the missing children, crewmen and passengers had been notified and news of the sinking released, though the name of the *Benares* was for the moment suppressed. For parents, it was the letter from Geoffrey Shakespeare that extinguished all hope. At Eastleigh, Freddie Steels's mother dreamed three nights running that she saw her son in a boat – and she told her husband so when she woke up. Going to the cinema to try to take her mind off her misery, she saw a sea drama during which Freddie's face kept smiling reassuringly at her out of the ocean. But when a message of sympathy arrived from Freddie's headmaster she sent his toys to be distributed among his classmates.

Ronnie Cooper's brother Ian (the family had five boys at sea) heard while at the convoy anchorage at Methil in the Firth of Forth of the sinking of the *Benares* long before the news was released. He telephoned his mother, saying simply: 'Ronnie is in danger and in need of your prayers.' She understood, and although at that stage she could get no confirmation from the shipping line, she did not neglect to pray.

Derek Capel's mother told a reporter: 'My husband, having witnessed the terrible destruction in London, thoroughly weighed up the question of sending the children away before finally making the decision. We both thought of their future, as well as their safety. The children were delighted at the prospect. They went away perfectly happy. Then came this terrible blow.'

Meanwhile, despite a freshening wind, Cooper continued under sail on that Sunday until 18.30, when frequent rain and hail squalls forced him to stop. They ran out the sea anchor again and rode to it stern first as before. The gale seemed to jeer at them with spiteful malevolence, and many times they were on the brink of disaster. To be tipped into the sea now, leaving no trace of their efforts to survive, was the unthinkable thought that tormented them.

The air was so cold that the hail formed in clusters on the gunwales, and when the sea calmed a little they hacked it off with frozen fingers and put it in their empty milk tins. It was little enough when melted down, but it provided a welcome supplement. They were never able to gather anything worthwhile from the rain.

Muscular spasms and claustrophobia induced by restriction of movement affected them all, and the boys felt as though bound and incarcerated, while many of the Lascars seemed too weak to move. For most of the time they lay in the bottom of the boat, though they still observed their religious rituals, rinsing out their mouths with sea water before prayer. How much they swallowed Cooper could never be sure. Certainly the torpor that affected the boys seemed accentuated in the Lascars, many of whom lapsed into a coma, their will to live waning. Some of the boys, too, were feverish, and they were encouraged to suck buttons and identity discs in an effort to salivate.

When the boys were favoured with an extra swig of water, the Lascars, suffering equal tortures, demanded similar treatment. The time for making sacrifices for the children, they indicated, was past. Because of their far greater numbers their pleas were resisted, but their resentment grew ominous. Cooper passed a hatchet up to O'Sullivan and asked him to flourish it if necessary, but the priest passed it to Mayhew, who kept it under his feet in the stern. He did not think the Lascars would become violent, and he joined with Ramjam in calming them down, directing what energy they possessed into prayer.

Throughout Monday they ran before a moderate wind, and late that afternoon, just before dusk, a long low smudge on the horizon which at first looked like a cloud eventually convinced them, after they had stared so hard that it hurt, that land lay ahead. As night fell they passed through another belt of phosphorescence, and in the midst of fitful sleep they saw flashes in the eastern sky and thought they heard gunfire. They longed for the daylight that would surely confirm what they believed must be true. But when dawn came, and they scanned the eastern horizon, the same leaden desert of ocean confronted them, with no trace of a landfall.

On Tuesday, 24 September, still eking out their meagre water supply, they completed a week in the lifeboat. They had seen nothing since the unidentified ship three days earlier, they had little idea how far they had travelled, and their strength was ebbing. They must reach land soon or perish.

Paul Shearing was so ill that Father O'Sullivan gathered

his diminishing strength to make an impassioned appeal. 'This child is dying. He must have water.' He was given enough to moisten his lips, that was all. Another of the boys became delirious, and his feet were so painful that he couldn't bear them to be massaged. During the night he raved spasmodically. 'I'm mad, I'm going mad, I know it!' He recovered his sanity with the coming of daylight.

At 13.00 on Wednesday, 25 September, their eighth day in the boat, Kenneth Sparks, the eldest of the boys, stood up to stretch his legs. Visibility was good and there was some welcome sunshine. Scouring sea and sky for some sign of possible rescue, he suddenly shouted wildly and pointed excitedly. 'There's a speck in the sky! Look! It's a plane!'

Those able to do so struggled to their feet, following the pointing finger. There was something there all right. Was it a bird or a plane? What chance was there that it would see them anyway? They had long since given up hope that anyone was looking for them. The ship hadn't seen them, why should the plane? And was it British or German? For all their fears they shouted in unison and waved arms and handkerchiefs and anything they could lay their hands on, knowing that such frenzied exertion was almost certainly wasted. Yet they did not desist – this without doubt was their last chance of rescue.

What they did not know was that this was no ordinary plane, in transit from one place to another, careless of its surroundings. Although the crew had completed their convoy escort duties and were on their way back to their base at Oban, they were automatically coupling their return flight with an anti-submarine patrol. So at least they were on the look-out.

'It's a Sunderland flying-boat!' shouted Ken Sparks, his

hours spent on aircraft recognition suddenly bearing fruit. 'It's an RAF plane! It's British!'

But how were they to attract the crew's attention, having used all their rockets? Suddenly everyone on board seemed to have the same inspiration: to use their empty milk tins as heliographs, flashing the sun's reflection at the flying-boat. Soon it turned towards them.

'Oh boy! We're going to fly home!' Within two or three minutes the plane was overhead, with someone signalling to them that they had been seen.

Father O'Sullivan reminded the boys of their promise, and now, with heads bent forward briefly, they joined hands to give thanks. None prayed more earnestly than the two boys who had been unavoidably parted from younger brothers. Both had sad news awaiting them.

The crew of the flying-boat – it was Sunderland D of 10 Squadron, Royal Australian Air Force, piloted by Squadron Leader W. H. Garing – had been airborne for many hours, having flown out into the Atlantic to escort incoming convoy HX 73. Their return route had chanced to take them within sight of the lifeboat, but although their margin of fuel was adequate for the patrol they had insufficient to see the rescue through to the end. But they were thrilled beyond measure when, from semaphore signals projected by Mayhew, they realized they were looking at forty-six survivors of the *City of Benares*.

After signalling by Aldis lamp that help would be coming, the Sunderland crew returned reluctantly to the convoy they had recently left and fulfilled their promise by passing on the details to the plane that had taken over from them half an hour earlier. This was Sunderland P9624 of 210 Squadron, piloted by Flight Lieutenant Ernest 'Doughie' Baker. With a ten-man crew and three supernumeraries, among them his squadron commander,

Wing Commander Francis Fressanges, Baker was not short of look-outs, and he set course for the position given him by the Australian crew. Fifteen minutes later, at 14.00, some forty-five miles from the convoy, the lifeboat was sighted, Cooper having meanwhile decided to lower sails and heave to.

A low-level circuit showed Baker that sea conditions would make it possible to alight on the water and take on the survivors if he had to, but he hoped to direct one of the convoy escort vessels to the scene. The flying-boat was travelling too fast for the crew to read the semaphore messages sent by Mayhew, but they filled a parachute bag with all the food and drink and cigarettes they had on board, added a smoke flare, and attached a life-jacket to the bag to keep it afloat. Mayhew grabbed the life-jacket and read the tie-on label attached to it. 'Help coming,' it said. 'Rescue vessel approximately 40 miles.' They would set off the flare when the rescue vessel came in sight.

Returning to the convoy, the Sunderland crew signalled the news to the senior officer of the escort, Lieutenant-Commander N. V. J. T. Thew of the destroyer HMS *Anthony*; 'Pugs' Thew was a New Zealander, and he undertook to fulfil the task himself. Baker also signalled his intention to rendezvous with the warship in two hours' time and home it on to the lifeboat if need be.

After watching HMS *Anthony* drop out of the convoy and head for the position given, Baker continued his anti-submarine patrol on the perimeter of the convoy. Finally he returned to keep the rendezvous with *Anthony*, only to find that the destroyer was some way off course. Signalling 'Follow me', Baker flew back and forth between warship and lifeboat, finally dropping a smoke flare which Thew saw and acknowledged. The Sunderland circled until 16.30, when the crew saw the warship make fast alongside the lifeboat; they took photographs of the scene. Ordered soon afterwards to return to base, they had rarely felt so bucked after a sortie.

The delay did not greatly disturb Cooper and his complement; they were feasting on their own and the Sunderland's provisions, draining every drop of juice and sauce out of the tins. Cooper refused to issue the last of the water – they were not rescued yet – but the change in their physical condition was amazing. Johnny Mayhew produced a mouth organ, and 'Tipperary' and 'Pack up Your Troubles' were sung.

It was Mayhew, too, who let off the smoke flare when they saw the destroyer. The *Anthony* signalled that she would come alongside, but Mayhew immediately sema-phored that the lifeboat would come to the *Anthony* rather than risk being capsized, asking her meanwhile to make still water. This the destroyer did by circling. Afterwards Lieutenant-Commander Thew wanted to meet the 19-year-old signaller who had countermanded his orders – but only to commend him for his seamanship.

Everyone in the lifeboat thought they would be able to scramble up the nets that the destroyer put down, but when the time came they were unable to do so. Sailors had to come down into the boat to help them, and most of them had to be carried aboard. As in *Hurricane*, the crew of *Anthony* did everything to welcome and succour the survivors, sacrificing their own clothing and comfort. And again as in *Hurricane*, the medical staff were much overworked, reporting twenty-six cot cases, and patients overflowed from the sick bay to all parts of the ship. None had suffered more severely than the Lascars, one of whom died during the night.

As in the lifeboat, language and cultural differences caused problems, aptly illustrated when the Lascars made a bonfire on *Anthony*'s deck of the bandages that had been wrapped round their frozen extremities and sat round it warming their feet.

At 19.00 the following evening, Thursday, 26 September, thirteen days after leaving Liverpool, the survivors were landed at Gourock. This, for Derek Capel, was another thirteen to add to an extraordinary sequence. In Glasgow they were fêted as heroes, and this applied with particular force to Mary Cornish and the boys – or rather five of them, since Paul Shearing was suffering so badly from trench-feet that he spent the next few weeks in hospital. Some of the Lascars, too, needed a lengthy recuperation, while Father O'Sullivan was not discharged from hospital until three months later. Nevertheless he enjoyed reading his obituary notice and thought it 'quite well written'.

The boys were entertained by the Provost of Glasgow and taken on a tour of the city, wearing the kilts that were presented to them to replace their lost clothing. Although accommodated in hospital, they were well enough to enjoy their fame, talking to the Press, being photographed, broadcasting on the radio and being filmed by the newsreels. Their relatives were sent for by the Corporation, and among the first to arrive were the parents of Billy and Peter Short. They had already been quoted as saying that the news was too good to be true. 'This gives us hope that Peter, too, may yet prove to be saved.' Similar hopes were raised among all the bereaved relatives, but sadly they proved false. There were to be no more miracles of survival. When Billy Short met his parents he had only one thought. 'Mummy, I have not got Peter for you.'

Friends called on Connie Peard in Bristol that night. 'Don't give up your hopes, Connie,' she was told. 'A boat has been found.' Sure enough the irrepressible Harry was in it. The Shearings received the news of Paul's survival in awed silence. 'A miracle has happened,' was how they explained their reaction, 'and we haven't had time to realize it yet.' Would Freddie Steels be allowed to try again? 'Never!' said his mother. The memorial service planned for Eastleigh Parish Church was switched to a service of Thanksgiving.

When Kenneth Sparks got back to Wembley, flags and bunting decorated his street and a crowd turned out to greet him.

Ronnie Cooper's mother felt her prayers had been answered. Doug Critchley rang his home soon after *Anthony* docked. 'It's me, Dad,' he said. 'Is that you, Doug?' came the amazed answer. 'We'd given you up.' Critchley senior brought his daughter to the phone to make sure the call wasn't a hoax. George Purvis's sister found greeting a brother whom she thought had been dead for a week the most eerie experience of her life.

Curiously enough, the boys talked much more freely about their hours on the destroyer than their days in the boat. Mixing with the crew of a real live warship was for them the climax of the adventure, and every one of them planned to join the Royal Navy when they grew up. Even more remarkably, most of them did.

Ronnie Cooper, George Purvis and Mary Cornish were all decorated, deservedly enough, and Ramjam too was rightly commended for his unswerving bravery and devotion to duty. But Bohdan Nagorski thought recognition should have been extended to a fifth member of the party, and for him he wrote his own citation.

Gunner Peard was full of energy and good humour the whole time; he found the best way to speak to the Lascars, and to more or less maintain their spirits, and although not a sailor he was always ready for any difficult job in the boat. In my opinion he contributed more than anyone else to the fact that, after eight hard days, we were found in a relatively good state, without having lost hope of rescue.

9

In Defence of the Lascars

Because of the alarming signal transmitted by *Hurricane* on the night of the rescue, which appeared to blame the Lascars for the extent of the *Benares* disaster, Geoffrey Shakespeare immediately recalled the thirty children who had already been embarked on the *City of Simla*, as previously recorded. The third Ellerman vessel with predominantly Lascar crews, the *City of Paris*, had sailed on 10 September for Cape Town and was beyond recall. However, a fourth and much bigger vessel, the *Llandaff Castle*, with 270 children, was due to sail for Cape Town on the 23rd. Meanwhile on the 20th the *Benares* survivors were landed and Shakespeare met and talked to the passengers and questioned the European crew. He was greatly relieved to find that the first reports received about the behaviour of the Lascar crew were not substantiated.

'I went straight to the bridge when the ship was torpedoed,' said Joe Hetherington, 'and when I got there the Lascar boat crews were at their stations and there was no sign of panic.' Third Officer Lee reported that the ship's emergency system had functioned correctly. There had been what he called 'a slight hitch' in the lowering, caused by the jamming of the after falls, but what had swamped his boat and washed oars and sails overboard was the violence of the seas. Ewan McVicar said his boat was launched correctly: 'The native crew behaved quite orderly and carried out my orders whilst getting the boat away.' (This was the unflooded Boat 4.) Barman Jimmie

Proudfoot, in one of the aft boats, saw many Lascars but no sign of panic; since the Lascars were accommodated aft, it was inevitable that they should crowd into the aft boats.

A crew member with responsibility for one of the forward boats, questioned about the alleged storming of boats by the Lascars, replied: 'I did not see any of this and am very sceptical.' Another said the Lascars behaved well. 'Only one was not manly.'

Evidence in support of the *Hurricane* signal, then, was not forthcoming from the crew. What happened was that the Lascars who were not on duty at the boat falls went straight to the boats to which they had been allotted and got in, with or without being specifically ordered to do so. They did not wait about, as many Europeans did, to let women and children go first; but this was a tradition with which the Europeans – but not the Lascars – had been indoctrinated almost from birth.

Some of the passengers, as Shakespeare found, remained critical of the Lascars, although one or two of the evacuee children – and there were only seven to give an opinion – actually praised them. Whether an all-European crew could have launched the boats more smoothly is an imponderable, but complaints about the behaviour of the Lascars in the boats, where in most cases they showed no further interest, were more difficult to refute. They wrapped themselves in the sails, it was said, offered no help to boat crews or comfort to the children, and gave up within a few hours, adding to the scenes of horror. While such reproaches might be said to reveal a lack of understanding and sympathy on the part of the Europeans, they were basically true. The Lascars displayed a lack of vitality in the boats which, it could be argued, should have been foreseen. What it had not been so easy to foresee, perhaps, were the extreme conditions to which they were exposed.

Eric Davis thought that whatever the competence of the crew might be, it would be heavily taxed under the conditions obtaining, and that it was unrealistic to expect too much from the Lascars. Hetherington assured Shakespeare that the Lascars had behaved very well on the ship and were good seamen. Hetherington, Purser Anderson, and the rest of the European crew all agreed that the conditions were such that no crew could have lowered the boats and kept them dry.

Shakespeare did not forget that the answers of the ship's officers might be inhibited by the need to protect themselves from charges of faults in leadership, but against this their professional pride was at stake. They would hardly admit their inability to cope without good reason.

Shakespeare also interviewed the managing director and the marine superintendent of the City Line, who told him that although five of their ships had been sunk since the war started there had been no previous complaints against the Lascars; indeed in one case they had been commended. Aware that even at this level ranks might be closed to hide deficiencies, Shakespeare looked for a more objective view and consulted the marine superintendent of the Royal Mail Line, a man of thirty years' experience. He confirmed the view that it would have been impossible in the circumstances described for anyone to keep the boats dry.

Meanwhile the most damning indictment, vehemently opposed to the majority view, had been addressed to Flag Officer i/c Greenock, and thence to the Admiralty, by Richard Deane. The main targets of his censure, however, were not the Lascars. The highly critical Deane had heard the tales on *Hurricane* of Lascars swarming down the ladders into boats further aft, but he himself had been in a boat amidships. 'I did not see it personally,' he admitted. Indeed, from his own account, four Lascars were the last to board his boat, presumably because they had stayed at their posts till the end. He had been glad to have them. Yet: 'I should have unhesitatingly shot any more Lascars had they attempted to come on board, but none did.' Such ruthlessness might have been justified if the rumours heard on *Hurricane* had been founded on fact, but Deane himself 'saw nothing to criticize in the behaviour of the Lascars'. He was clearly a man who would have spoken out fearlessly had he thought it was warranted.

Nevertheless, having admitted that he was giving hearsay evidence, Deane repeated in his report what he called the 'frightful stories' of Lascars capsizing boats in their panic and throwing children out to make room for themselves. 'How much truth there is in this I cannot say, but certainly frightful screams were coming from the after end of the ship before she went down.' These screams emanated from boats where falls had jammed and whole boatloads were thrown into the sea, as Eric Davis confirmed. 'I saw no sign of panic. The only cries of distress came from those tipped into the water.'

Deane was fair-minded enough to concede that the stories he'd heard might well be the outpourings of hysteria, but he went on to deliver a swingeing attack on the state of the life-saving apparatus and emergency crew drill on the *Benares*. 'I say that in the conditions under which the ship was sunk, with a properly trained crew and efficient lifeboats, there should have been no loss of life.' This view, if substantiated, would have implicated not only Ellerman's but the Ministry of Shipping as well.

Deane wrote all this in the heat of the moment while he was still aboard *Hurricane*, with his own grief at the loss of his wife still preying on his mind; but there is no evidence that he ever retracted it. And he followed it with strictures which, in the days that followed, found more support. 'That children should have been given passage on a ship manned by Lascars is to my mind a terrible blunder . . . Had I known previously that this was a ship in the Eastern trade manned by Lascars I would not have booked on her.'

This, on the face of it, constituted an unsupported smear against a respected ethnic group which suggested the worst kind of racial prejudice. But the unfortunate Lascars, having been more or less acquitted of the two major charges – poor seamanship during the launching, and rushing the boats – were sadly vulnerable to the charge that they had been a liability in the boats. Martin Bum blamed three factors for the deaths of thirteen children in his boat: heavy seas, light clothing, and a complete lack of assistance from the Lascar crew. Marjorie Day, the senior escort, who watched thirteen children die in her boat, told Shakespeare: 'Never should British children be sent to sea with a Lascar crew. It was disastrous.' But she added: 'Otherwise I have nothing but good to say of the ship.' Few would have expected Asian seamen to compare with their European counterparts in the conditions obtaining, yet failing in this was the sin for which they were now being condemned.

Meanwhile Shakespeare was in a dilemma. The process of informing next of kin was not yet completed and the news of the sinking had not been released to the Press. What was he to do about the *Llandaff Castle* and the 270 children waiting to embark?

On 21 September, he learned that the *City of Simla* had

been sunk within twenty-four hours of sailing, which did not encourage him. On the other hand, the news that there had been only two casualties, both killed in the explosion, that the boats had been launched without mishap, and that all the survivors had been rescued, tended to confirm all he'd been told. Under normal conditions – and the weather had been good – the efficiency of Lascar crews was undoubted. But the ship had still been under escort, and the incident bore no comparison with the sinking of the *City of Benares*, so it did not help him in his decision.

Although the companies who employed Lascar crews spoke so highly of them, Shakespeare was coming round to the conclusion that it would be better not to send children in ships where Lascars formed a major part of the crew, even when there was adequate European supervision – as he believed there had been on the *City of Benares*. Here he was accepting one of two propositions, or perhaps both: one, that more children might have been saved – that is, survived in the boats – had the entire *Benares* crew been European; or two, that parents might think this was so, even if it was not.

Another factor that influenced him was the deception he felt he would be practising on parents if he allowed the *Llandaff Castle* to sail with 270 children before the news of the loss of the *Benares* was made public: he would be denying parents the chance to withdraw their children if they wished to do so in the light of that catastrophe. If he took no action, and disaster befell the ship and its complement, parents would have a real grievance against the Board for being in possession of information which in all good faith should have been imparted to them in time for them to change their minds if they wished.

For these reasons, and believing that there would have

to be a full investigation into the circumstances of the loss of life in the *Benares* before further sailings were contemplated, Shakespeare disembarked the children from the *Llandaff Castle*.

In a report to his Board dated 22 September, the day the news of the sinking was released, Shakespeare emphasized these points. He then considered what the future policy should be. 'On the one hand is the delightful welcome and home life awaiting our children, free from the war atmosphere and particularly the nervous effects and discomfort of air raids. On the other hand, the risks of achieving this seem latterly to be increasing . . . It will not be possible to launch boats safely in conditions of gale and Atlantic swell common to the winter months.' His recommendations to the Board were:

1 To send children only in ships with European Crews.
2 To announce the suspension of sponsored evacuation on the North Atlantic route during the winter months, except in the case of fast escorted liners.
3 To continue sending children to the other three Dominions, provided convoys were available.

Meanwhile the Ministry of Shipping was continuing to take written depositions from members of the crew and selected passengers, and on 21 September they pre-empted Shakespeare with the following ruling: 'It appears desirable that any further use of ships manned with Lascars for conveying children who are being evacuated under official auspices should be avoided. Pending a decision, no more children will be booked on such ships.' This effectively halted the official evacuation of children across the Atlantic for the time being. When all the depositions were available – 'as soon as possible', requested the Minister on 21 September – he would consider whether a Formal Investigation under the Merchant Shipping Acts, parts of which might have to be held *in camera*, should be ordered. His impression was that, in view of the heavy loss of life and the publicity the case had received, such an investigation would be desirable.

The Admiralty, who had the benefit, if such it was, of Deane's report, were of the same opinion: if that report were substantiated, there must have been something seriously wrong with the organization in the *City of Benares* and in the state of her life-saving appliances. But the Minister of Shipping wanted to see the depositions first, and he refused to be rushed into a decision.

10

'It will never be known'

On 2 October, despite protests from all sides, both home and overseas, that the CORB scheme was an admirable one and should not be abandoned because of one setback, the government announced its suspension. 'The recent sinking of vessels carrying children overseas,' said a Downing Street statement (only one such vessel had actually been sunk), 'has illustrated the dangers to which passenger vessels are exposed, even when in convoy, under the weather conditions now prevailing in the Atlantic.' (The weather was getting the blame, which was a supportable view; but whether the *Benares* was technically in convoy once the escort had left will be examined.) The government had reluctantly decided that until further notice no more children would be sent under the CORB scheme, though private bookings were not affected. The keen disappointment this would cause overseas was recognized and warm thanks were expressed to 'the very many people in the Dominions and the United States' who had so generously offered hospitality to children from the vulnerable areas of Great Britain. The question of whether operations might be resumed in the following year would turn on the conditions then prevailing.

The first depositions had got the departmental enquiry at the Ministry of Shipping off to a soothing start. 'These [depositions] do not support the allegations in the first telegram received to the effect that all the boats were rushed by Lascars and capsized,' said the Ministry. But the Admiralty, with Deane's report in mind, were pressing for a full enquiry. 'There are too many questions on this disaster being asked in the country to allow it to pass without further investigation.'

One of the most pertinent questions was put by the *Times Educational Supplement*. '. . . there is bound to be a certain amount of uneasiness which can never be completely allayed until it is known officially why 139 adults out of 316 were saved, but only 13 out of 90 children . . . In the interests of all, a full-length official enquiry at the earliest possible moment is obligatory.'

On the day the CORB scheme was suspended, the First Lord, A. V. Alexander, expressed the view to Ronald Cross, Minister of Shipping, that a full enquiry should be held. With this communication he attached a copy of Deane's report, but he took the precaution of excising the last paragraph, which read:

When did our escort leave us and why did they not return to pick us up? In other words, why had we to wait while HMS *Hurricane* steamed some 280 miles in a sea in which she could not make her top speed when it would seem that the two escort vessels [in fact there had been three] must have been very much nearer? Sixteen hours seems to have been an excessive time before rescue ships could come to the scene.

Indeed so. If a vessel could have got to the scene more quickly, many more lives would have been saved. But the Admiralty, while passing on Deane's other criticisms, did not want to encourage such speculation – though they consistently maintained that *Hurricane* was the nearest vessel at the time of the sinking.

In his report Deane fulminated against the station-keeping of the ships in the convoy; they straggled, he said, all over the place. 'Sometimes we were the leading ship in the centre, sometimes ships were ahead of us on one bow or another, and quite often two or three ships were straggling along two or three miles astern.' This brought him to a controversial point, one raised by several others: 'Surely if a ship is carrying evacuee children it should be put in the centre of the convoy, masked by the other seventeen or eighteen ships in proper formation.'

The Admiralty did not censor this criticism, nor did they answer it, although the responsibility for the make-up and configuration of convoys was theirs. The position-ing of other vessels in the convoy to form a shield might perhaps have proved incompatible with the role of *Ben-ares* as commodore ship, but the point was never made. As for station-keeping, HMS *Winchelsea* reported that in OB 213 it had been average for lightly-loaded ships oper-ated by crews of widely differing nationalities; it was felt that in view of the weather they did quite well.

Meanwhile queries on the suitability of the Lascars for the Atlantic route were put down for Question Time in the House of Commons, the Under-Secretary of State for Dominions Affairs (Geoffrey Shakespeare) being asked

in what circumstances and on whose responsibility the *City of Benares*, manned by Lascars unsuited to the cold Atlantic route, was chartered to convey children who were being evacuated to Canada; and if he would give an assurance that, on the evacua-tion of children being resumed, vessels and crews familiar with and suited to the appropriate routes will be chartered and chosen respectively.

Shakespeare managed to work in a defence of the Lascars into his answer without actually mentioning them, and he also kept his options open for the future. 'The conditions were such that it was very difficult to launch the boats without water being shipped . . . the possibility of using vessels regularly running on the respective routes will be carefully borne in mind.'

Shakespeare was still puzzled by an aspect of the tragedy that worried many. 'I understood from the Admiralty,' he wrote, 'that in a convoy one or two ships were told off to act as rescue ships and were charged with the duty of stopping to rescue survivors of any ship that was torpedoed.' This had been the understanding of everyone at CORB from the start. Rescue ships had stopped to pick up survivors of the *Volendam* three weeks previously; why hadn't one of the ships that had been dimly visible from the *Benares* gone to the rescue? On at least one ship, eye-witnesses actually saw children being tipped out of the boats.

As the departmental enquiry at the Ministry of Shipping progressed, digging out many unpalatable facts, enthusiasm for a Formal Investigation waned, and on 28 November the Minister was advised that although the loss of 256 lives in a marine disaster in peacetime would certainly have been followed by a public enquiry, if only to satisfy the public that all possible measures for the safety of life at sea had been taken, the loss of the *City of Benares* was 'a war casualty resulting from Germany's unrestricted warfare at sea, and the essential facts were clear'. The first-named culprit had been the weather; now it was nobody's fault but the Germans'. The unanimous opinion of the Minister's staff now was that a formal public enquiry was not necessary. In support of their conclusion, which they forwarded to the Admiralty and the Dominions Office, they cited the following factors:

The results of the survey and inspection before sailing.
The careful consideration given beforehand to the use of an Indian crew.

The daily boat drills that had been held on board (except once when the weather was bad).

The launching problems that were not uncommon in bad weather.

The absence of any evidence of panic on the part of the children, passengers or crew.

The loss of life had been caused primarily by the torpedoing of the vessel and the swamping of the boats followed by eighteen hours' exposure in the boats in severe weather.

By listing these points the Ministry sought to absolve themselves from blame. But on the principle that attack was the best defence, they reminded the agencies concerned of matters which might cause them embarrassment in turn in the event of a public enquiry. First the Admiralty: they would doubtless give consideration to two particular points – one, that none of the vessels in the convoy had been instructed to go to the rescue if the children's ship was sunk, and two, that after the escort had left, the convoy had continued in formation at the restricted convoy speed, in contravention of the orders given to the commodore before sailing, while the signal to scatter had not been given until after the children's ship had been torpedoed. Next the Dominions Office: many of the children had been inadequately clad; they had not been sleeping in their day clothes, as ordered by the chief officer.

First to react, ten days later, was Shakespeare: he agreed that a public enquiry was not necessary. He accepted that Hetherington had advised the children to sleep in their day clothes, and that his order had never been countermanded by captain or crew. So it must have been rescinded by the escorts. But he held that it was not a factor that had materially affected their chances of survival. 'Many of the escorts who were fully clothed perished.' He would hardly have got away with this at an official enquiry. If only one child had survived through being fully clothed it would have been worth it.

Shakespeare then turned to the points that had been put to the Admiralty. He would have preferred that ships had been told off as rescue ships in case of enemy action or accident, but he thought that whether ships were safer dispersed or in a group once escorts had left was a matter of opinion – arguments could be adduced both ways.

The Admiralty took their time to reply, but when they did, on 20 December, they were persuaded that there was no need for an enquiry. As for the complaints that might be lodged against them, they quoted the orders that had been in force at the time for rescuing survivors of other vessels:

1 Whenever other considerations permit the rear ships of columns should be detailed to act as Rescue Ships for their respective columns.
2 Rescue Ships may go to the assistance of vessels damaged by enemy action *when a local escort is present* [Admiralty's italics]. If the local escort is not present a Rescue Ship should not act unless this can be done without undue risk.

This meant that, in effect, when the *Benares* lost the protection of the escort it also lost the safeguard of the detailed rescue ships. It was this double blow that sealed the children's fate.

As for the point that the *Benares*, because of the children, might have been treated as an exception, the Admiralty countered: 'We do not think it would have been proper to depart from the above orders on account of the children . . . as this would possibly have endangered another ship.' This bleak dismissal of any special

moral responsibility for the evacuee children would surely
have caused a scandal had it been known.

It was an attitude that was later discountenanced by
Admiral Nasmith, who incredibly had been left in ignorance of the nature of the *Benares* payload. On 5 October
1940 he asked the Admiralty to keep him informed of any
such special payloads in future 'in order that appropriate
measures for their security may be taken'. The inference
was that he would somehow have strengthened the escort
or its radius of action, or given special orders for rescue
ships, had he been told. Accepting the rebuke, the
Admiralty signalled all ports under Nasmith's control,
copied to Nasmith: 'The names of ships carrying passengers or cargo of special value, whether sailing independently or in ocean convoys, are to be reported to C.-in-C.
Western Approaches, as long notice as possible being
given.'

As for Mackinnon's failure to disperse the convoy in
accordance with his instructions, the Admiralty confessed
that they did not know why he had acted as he had. 'As
he most unfortunately went down with the ship, it will
never be known.' Hadn't the chief officer or some other
officer been taken into Mackinnon's and Nicoll's confidence? Apparently not. They went on: 'The First Lord
feels, therefore, that nothing would be gained from a
public enquiry into the Naval aspects of the circumstances
in which this vessel was lost.'

Should an announcement be made of the decision not
to hold an enquiry, asked the Ministry of Shipping? The
Admiralty, on the principle of 'least said soonest
mended', didn't think so. That was to be hushed up as
well. 'It appears to us that the balance of advantage would
probably lie in saying nothing . . . So far as we know, the
public disquiet at the sinking of this vessel is now dying

down and any further announcement, and particularly one saying we do not propose to hold a public enquiry, might well revive feelings that can only lead to unprofitable recrimination.'

While satisfied with the Admiralty's conclusion that no enquiry should be held or statement made, the Minister of Shipping was not disposed to let the Admiralty so easily off the hook. He remarked on the complete failure to explain why no ship of any sort reached the scene of the disaster for sixteen hours, and queried whether it was reasonable in the circumstances for the commodore to have kept the convoy assembled for ten hours after it should have been dispersed. Did the Admiralty think it advisable to impress on commodores the importance of complying with their instructions in this matter?

The Admiralty fielded this one as best they could, falling back on naval tradition.

We rather doubt whether anything would be gained by emphasizing to commodores of convoys the need for adherence to instructions about dispersal. They are all of considerable experience, and would realize the importance of complying with their orders unless there was some strong overriding reason for not doing so which could not have been foreseen when the instructions were drawn up. In such an uncertain business as convoy work in wartime a certain latitude must be left to the man on the spot.

What, in the case of Admiral Mackinnon, was the strong overriding reason? The Admiralty did not venture to suggest one. Couldn't Joe Hetherington throw any light at all on what took place between Mackinnon and Nicoll? Apparently not. 'We have in fact tried to find out from survivors,' replied the Admiralty, 'including both the chief officer and the fourth officer, why the commodore disregarded his instructions to disperse at noon on the 17

September but no information could be obtained on this point.'

Survivors from other ships in Convoy OB 213 say it was quite common practice for commodores to keep ships together until the convoy was actually located by the enemy. The theory was that, in the vastness of the Atlantic, a single group of ships moving together reduced the number of positions where a ship might be found. Since the Admiral must have known perfectly well that no ship was likely to stop if his own was torpedoed, this must have been his reasoning. But as with the rigidity of Admiralty orders, it took no account of the special cargo carried by his ship.

Post-war examination of Bleichrodt's log points strongly to the conclusion that had Admiral Mackinnon obeyed his orders the *City of Benares* would have escaped. After firing his last bow torpedoes at the liner and at the freighter *Marina*, Bleichrodt loitered briefly to witness results, as we have seen. But after the convoy dispersed, and seven minutes before the *Benares* sank, he turned to bring his after tube to bear on a medium-sized tanker. As he did so the tanker crew, alerted by the sinkings, sighted him in the moonlight and opened fire.

Bleichrodt was forced to break off, but he began to haul ahead of the tanker for another attempt. The tanker had meanwhile begun a zigzag course, against a strong sea and at a speed of 10 knots, and it wasn't until nearly three hours later that Bleichrodt attained what he regarded as a suitable attacking position. Then, as he ran in, and just as he was about to fire, the tanker altered course again and disappeared in a rain squall. Ten minutes later Bleichrodt found his quarry again and began to haul ahead for a fresh attack, but the tanker, continuing to zigzag, vanished once more in another rain squall. This was the last Bleichrodt saw of her or of any other ships in what was now a widely dispersed convoy. Scattering, and the magnet of a passenger liner, had saved all but the *Marina*.

Certainly the tanker crew had been alerted by the sinkings. But if the *Benares* had been sailing alone she too would have been zigzagging; she had only stopped doing so because of the danger of collision. With her 15 knots, against the tanker's 10, she should have been safe.

In seeking to avoid the full enquiry which they themselves had once regarded as essential, the Admiralty and the Ministry of Shipping were greatly assisted by the proliferation of wartime incident which diverted public interest in the winter of 1940–1. The stoical resignation of many parents was not untypical of the 'if it's got my name on it' philosophy of the period, but the incident played a part, however unjustly, in the deep-rooted hatred of the Nazis that developed that winter, stiffening national resolve and helping to unite world opinion behind Britain.

Since nothing could bring the children back, the forbearance of parents was understandable. But others harboured lasting resentments. 'I shall not forgive or forget,' wrote Hugh Crofton Simms in a letter home soon after the sinking; and he added, 'I do not ask them to do so either to me.' And to Purser John Anderson he wrote: 'In the meantime, let us go on against these foes with neither mercy nor quarter henceforth.' From this point on his pursuit of the enemy was relentless, and after HMS *Hurricane* had been hit in a bombing raid on Liverpool Docks in May 1941 he and most of his crew were transferred to another destroyer in the Atlantic Battle, where in one 36-hour period they sank three enemy submarines.

Promoted in July 1942 to commander, having by then

earned a DSO and two mentions in despatches, Simms was given command that September of the corvette HMS *Snapdragon* and appointed leader of an escort group engaged in hazardous coastal operations in the Mediterranean. His selfless dedication to the task in hand inevitably increased his exposure, and the end came for him in December 1942, when he was mortally wounded in an air attack on his ship.

For some, bitterness was directed nearer home. Doug Critchley felt that the way *Benares* stayed in unescorted convoy for twenty-one hours was unforgivable. 'It was a senseless, pointless blunder.' John Anderson felt the loss was quite unnecessary – the *Benares* should have been steaming alone at top speed. 'It was just a case of the U-boats biding their time and picking us off.' Marjorie Day wrote: 'The children hadn't a chance . . . What is needed is escort by warship over a longer period. We were an absolute sitter for any submarine crew that had the intelligence to wait till our escort left us.' (Naval escort for the entire Atlantic crossing was not available until mid-1941.) Pat Fletcher of *Hurricane* wrote: 'It seems to be a very bad principle to send children out in a slow convoy.'

Ellerman's seem not to have been consulted during the departmental investigation, but they were sent a copy of the Ministry of Shipping memorandum summarizing the information contained in the depositions. The Ministry 'found some evidence to show that some of the Lascars were inefficient in lowering the boats', and they also mentioned their apathy once in the boats. There were references, too, to the undressing of the children, the confusion among passengers as to whether they should proceed direct to their boats or to their muster stations, and to faults that had been reported in the boat equipment.

Ellerman's replied that they had already made 'the closest enquiry' into all the circumstances attaching to the loss and were glad to be able to assure the Ministry that 'our firm were lacking in no respect'. They cited experience in the *City of Simla* as confirming that bad weather conditions had been mainly responsible for the difficulties encountered in launching. They quoted Hetherington's recommendation that all passengers sleep in their clothes and that the children wear life-jackets even in bed, and argued that they could not be held responsible if these instructions were not carried out. 'Some little blame', they thought, 'may be attached to the escorts.' Hetherington's instructions to the passengers, they claimed, had been perfectly clear and well rehearsed, and any deficiencies in boat equipment were explained by damage caused by the explosion or during the launching. The Ministry decided that on balance they had no reason to doubt the high standards claimed by Ellerman's. Bad weather had been mainly responsible.

One point that emerged from the depositions, although it appears to have gone unnoticed, was that only one of the boat drills ordered after the *City of Benares* sailed was attended by the crew as a whole; the others had been drills for passengers attended by off-duty personnel only. But the crew had taken part in the drills before sailing, and it would have been impracticable for them to practise lowering and launching at sea in bad weather. So despite Deane's criticisms, Ellerman's emerged unscathed.

One innovation, welcomed by all merchant seamen, was inspired by the disaster. 'Arrangements have been made', the Admiralty told the Ministry of Shipping on 20 December, 'to supply special Rescue Ships.' The primary role of escort vessels was counter-attack, and when rear ships in convoys stopped to pick up survivors they were all too often torpedoed themselves. The outcome, as on the *Benares*, was that the shipwrecked were left to fend for themselves. Directly as a result of the loss of the *Benares*, a scheme was envisaged in November 1940 for the introduction of a new type of Rescue Ship whose sole purpose would be the rescue of shipwrecked seamen. Since ocean-going ships capable of carrying cargo could not be spared, the choice fell on small coasting vessels of around 1,500 tons whose peacetime role had scarcely taken them out of sight of land. However, their high manoeuvrability and low freeboard fitted them well for the task of picking up survivors from the water, and in practice they proved at least as ocean-worthy as many ships twice their size. Their numbers never averaged more than twelve, but by the end of the war they had saved over 4,000 lives. In the nature of things, they came too late to save the children whose deaths had inspired their introduction.

With hindsight it seems clear that the torpedoing of the *Volendam* was a warning that should have been heeded, leading to the abandonment of further transportation of children on the Atlantic route. Instead, at a time when the scheme was at last functioning successfully, there was a natural tendency to view the *Volendam* incident as a welcome reassurance that escorts and other ships in a convoy could cope. Yet Britain's rising losses at sea, which exceeded 100,000 tons in the week ending 25 August for the first time, might well have caused the authorities to pause. Churchill had drawn attention to these losses, and the Admiralty and the Ministry of Shipping knew, even if Shakespeare didn't, that U-boats were ranging far out into the Atlantic, beyond the limit of escort. But that a halt should have been called is easy to say with the knowledge of hindsight: no one knew then that the German plan for the invasion of Britain was about to be pigeon-holed, and that the blitz, severe as it was for the whole of that winter, was to tail off in the spring, never to be renewed on a comparable scale.

The effect on the survivors seems to have been less traumatic than might be imagined. Both *Hurricane* and *Anthony* proved outstandingly fruitful recruiting bases, all the boys forming ambitions to join the Navy and most of them eventually doing so, while at least one of the girl survivors joined the WRNS. Colin Ryder Richardson suffered more than most from the experience, which is not surprising in so sensitive a child, yet he told his mother when she met him in Glasgow: 'I want to join the Navy, Mum, and be a sailor.' Through interruption to his schooling on medical advice he failed the Dartmouth examination when the time came, but he did his National Service in the Navy.

After reading that George Medals were available for children, Professor Day wrote to Lord Chatfield, Chairman of the Civil Defence Honours Committee, with an account of Colin's conduct. 'Apart from Colin's merit,' he reasoned, 'the authorities might have been glad to recognize the courage and conduct of the many children who went so pathetically and trustingly to their death, in a vessel abandoned by the naval escort in dangerous waters.' Such a gesture to one of the surviving children, as representative of them all, or perhaps posthumously to George Crawford, the Sunderland boy so highly praised by Eleanor Wright ('George was a hero'), would surely have been appropriate and much appreciated by parents. Eventually, on 7 January 1941, the *London Gazette* recorded a King's Commendation for Colin: he was commended, it was said, for 'brave conduct in the Merchant Navy' – surely the youngest-ever recipient of such an honour.

Had tragedy not overtaken the children during and after launching, many of the *Benares* crew must have received awards. Hetherington and Asher were launching life-rafts until just before the ship went down, and Asher did not survive. Many passengers paid tribute to the work of crew members in the boats. For her cool resourcefulness and soothing influence at her muster station, in her lifeboat and on *Hurricane*, stewardess Annie Ryan also received a King's Commendation.

'I have been informed', wrote the Receiver of Wreck from Glasgow to the Australian Arthur Dowling, 'that you behaved with great heroism at the time of the casualty and I would appreciate it if you could see your way to call and make a statement on oath.' But this 'big tough guy', as his fellow passengers called him, put off perhaps by the preamble to the invitation, modestly excused himself on the grounds of fatigue. Not even the Press could persuade him to talk.

Joe Hetherington told his employees of five crew members whom he thought deserving of special praise. One was Annie Ryan; a second was First Radio Officer Alistair Fairweather, 'who, by standing by his post of duty and radiating the distress message was the means of the rescue ship locating the survivors', and who 'showed his total disregard of danger and thus set a high example of devotion to duty which cost him his life'. (The second radio officer, Canadian John Lazarus, also perished.) The others commended by Hetherington were three Lascars: Ramjam in Boat 12, Deck Serang Raimoodun Samsoodun in Alex Macauley's boat, and captain's boy Abdool

Soban, 'whose assistance to passengers during the launching and cheerful willingness in his lifeboat had set an admirable example to his fellows'. Sadly the cold eventually overcame Abdool and he died of exposure before *Hurricane* arrived.

Beth Cummings and Bess Walder were satisfied to escape with their lives, and they looked back on their ordeal as formative in a positive way: they benefited from it in increased confidence and an enhanced perspective. Every day that followed was a bonus. The friendship they developed in *Benares*, when they swore to stick together, has lasted ever since, cemented and extended in 1947 when Bess married Beth's brother.

The Bech and Choat children recovered fully, as did Tony Quinton, now Lord Quinton, Chairman of the British Library. Jack Keeley and John Baker impress as being of an indestructible mould.

There was one more award arising from the sinking of the *City of Benares*, and that went to Heinrich Bleichrodt, who received from Hitler the Knight's Cross with Oak Leaves for one of the most successful cruises of the war. Bleichrodt's war record of twenty-four ships sunk, totalling 151,319 tons, placed him high on the list of successful U-boat commanders. He survived the war and died in 1977.

So far as Bleichrodt and other U-boat commanders were concerned, sinking ships was their job, a point that was generally conceded after the war. Only one U-boat commander was prosecuted, and his offence was firing on survivors, for which he and his officers were tried, found guilty and executed. This incident placed Grand Admiral Doenitz, who by that time was commanding the German Navy as a whole, in some jeopardy at the war crimes trial at Nuremberg, and although there was a strong Allied naval lobby which held that he had fought an honourable war, there were other charges against him. The indictment included the sinking of the *City of Benares*. 'The point to be emphasized,' said the British prosecutor, 'is not the unusual brutality of the attack, but rather that such results are inevitable when a belligerent disregards the rules of sea warfare.' (The British, of course, knew of this disregard when they despatched the children.) However, of all the Nazi war leaders, Doenitz escaped with the lightest sentence – ten years. Decisive in his favour was an affidavit by Admiral Chester Nimitz, of the United States Navy, in which he declared: 'As a general rule United States submarines did not rescue enemy survivors if by doing so the vessels were exposed to unnecessary or additional risk.'

Having successfully organized the passage overseas of 2,662 sponsored children, 1,530 to Canada, 577 to Australia, 202 to New Zealand, and 353 to South Africa, and seen 838 go to the United States under Marshall Field's United States Committee for the Care of European Children, the Children's Overseas Reception Board was disbanded, a small staff being retained with responsibility for those children already evacuated, while Geoffrey Shakespeare returned to his desk in the Dominions Office. Strangely enough, however, the most important moral question raised by the disaster of the *Benares*, emphasized by *The Times* in a leader on 23 November 1940, was never pursued. Were the assurances given to parents on the extent to which their children would be protected from enemy action fully honoured?

The letter to parents from CORB had been quite specific: the government could not take responsibility for sending children overseas under the scheme without adequate naval protection. When parents received notification that their child had been accepted and placed on a waiting list, they could 'conclude that the ship in which [their] child (or children) was to sail *would be convoyed*'. (Author's italics.) If at the very last moment there were to be a sudden change in the situation and the Admiralty informed the Board that the ship could not, after all, be convoyed, '*the arrangements for the sailing would be cancelled forthwith*' and parents would be notified. (The Board's italics.)

What did the word 'convoyed' mean? It was no answer to say that the *Benares* was still with the convoy when she was sunk. Was she being convoyed?

'Two requirements must be fulfilled before ships can be said to be sailing in convoy,' wrote the Admiralty historian later. 'They must be operating in an organized group and they must be provided with an escort.' At the time of the sinking, the first of these requirements was being fulfilled, the second was not. The *City of Benares* was not being convoyed when she was sunk.

Had parents known that the limit of convoy in that period of the war was 17 degrees West, and that U-boats were known in recent weeks to be operating farther out in the Atlantic than that, they would have expected to be told that sailings were cancelled. If the Board didn't actually cancel the sailing (on the advice of the Admiralty), at least they would have been expected to give parents the opportunity to withdraw their children.

That Geoffrey Shakespeare himself accepted this principle was illustrated when he disembarked thirty children from the *City of Simla* after the *Benares* sinking and later withdrew another 270 from the *Llandaff Castle* – because there was no time to consult parents about their wishes.

When the news of the sinking was released, no attempt was made to suppress the fact that the escort had left the convoy some time earlier; it would indeed have been impossible to suppress it, otherwise the hiatus before rescue would have been inexplicable. But it was stated by Shakespeare in mitigation that no U-boat attack had developed this far out in the Atlantic before, and that the *City of Benares* had reached waters hitherto regarded as safe. But just as Shakespeare was left in the dark about the orders to other ships in the convoy not to stop if it involved them in risk, so he seems to have been ignorant of the succession of U-boat attacks, starting in the last ten days of August, which had sunk several ships at a similar distance from land. The area was in fact far from safe.

The answer to the question raised when the news of the sinking was released as to 'whether the ships had been convoyed far enough out to sea' was clearly no. And in the weeks that followed, while the depositions were being taken and the ministries concerned were seeking to avoid a formal investigation, letters written to newspapers, although not published and even possibly censored, showed that public disquiet still smouldered. Correspondence reaching The *Times Educational Supplement*, for instance, showed that the minds of bereaved parents remained 'grievously troubled', as a *Times* leader put it, over the discrepancy between the expectation of a continuous escort and the facts since established. 'They question whether the guarantee, implicit or explicit, on the strength of which they let their children go, was in the event fulfilled, and whether they ought not to have been given the opportunity of cancelling the passage taken.'

After a brief acknowledgement that the requirements of security might provide decisive reasons why public discussion should be avoided, *The Times* suggested a direct approach and explanation to the bereaved. 'Though the most conclusive answer cannot undo a lifelong grief, the Ministers concerned will, to say the least of it, be well advised to find a way of taking these parents most thoroughly into their confidence.'

But they never did. Parents had been promised that their children would be convoyed, and that promise had been broken. There was nothing anyone could say.

Appendix 1
Final Table of Losses

	Total	Lost	Percentage
European Crew	43	20	46.5
Asian Crew	166	101	60.5
Convoy Staff	6	3	50
Passengers (Fare-paying)	91	51	56
CORB Escorts	10	6	60
CORB Children	90	77	85.5
	406	258	

The crew figures were distorted by the disproportion of Asians to Europeans in Boat 12: 32 (of whom one died after rescue) against 2. But for that disproportion, the ratio of losses among Asian crew against European crew would have been substantially higher than it was.

Appendix 2
Note on Sources

Survivors

John Baker, Derek Capel, Doug Critchley, Bess Cummings (née Walder), Norma Jacoby, Jack Keeley, John McGlashan, Johnny Mayhew, Rev. Rory O'Sullivan, Barbara Partridge (née Bech), the late Harry Peard, James Proudfoot, Lord Quinton, Colin Ryder Richardson, Anne Seville (née Ryan), Paul Shearing, Fred Steels, Rachel Taylor (née Choat), Beth Williams (née Cummings), Sonia Williams (née Bech).

Relatives of casualties, and of survivors no longer alive

Maureen Clay, I. R. Cooper, Major R. Fleetwood-Hesketh, Mabel Geddes (née Anderson), Fred Grimmond, Theodora Lang (née Carr), Mrs B. Macauley, Doug Macdonald, Margaret M. Nicoll, Maureen S. Oldfield (née Walsh), Mrs H. de Vere Packe (née Deane), Rosemary Proctor (née Rennie), Anita Rose (née Hurwitz), Anice Shepherd (née Nicoll), Lillian Spencer-Davies, Mrs F. Templeton, Tom Williams.

Depositions and reports of survivors submitted at the time

John H. Anderson (Purser), Dr Martin Bum, Ronald M. Cooper (Fourth Officer), Eric Davis, Professor J. P. Day, Marjorie E. Day (Senior Children's Escort), Lt-Cdr R. T. Deane, RNVR, R. Hetherington (Chief Officer), W. J. Lee (Third Officer), N. Lewis (Chief Officer, *Marina*), Alex Macauley (Chief Engineer), Colin B. Macdonald (Supernumerary Chief Engineer), John McGlashan (Second

Engineer), Ewan McVicar (Carpenter), Bohdan Nagorski, Captain R. T. Paine (Master of the *Marina*), Captain
J. P. Webster (Master of the *Volendam*).

HMS Hurricane

Dr Peter Collinson, Patrick Fletcher, Fred Wiles, BEM.

HMS Anthony

R. de L. Brooke, DSO, DSC.

Public Record Office

Among the many files consulted at the Public Record
Office at Kew, the following were the most relevant:
Admiralty Files ADM 199/23, 50, 51, 142, 144, 1707, 2134
and 2213, ADM 223/148; Air Ministry Files AIR 24/374,
AIR 27/149 and 1298; Dominion Office Files DO131/1, 2,
20, 21, 79–81, 88–92; Ministry of Transport Files MT9/
3406, 3461.

Other sources

Arbroath Library; Barbara Britton; Gus Britton, Royal
Navy Submarine Museum; Harold Brough and Howard
Davis, *Liverpool Daily Post and Echo*; Robin Corfield;
T. P. Cox; Ellerman City Lines (Noel Kent, Public
Relations); Kathleen Everest; Falkirk High School, Form
2 (1984–5); Richard Gaunt, of PR Solutions, and Laura
Douglas; Glasgow University Archives (Research Assist-
ant Alma Topen); Leslie V. Huyton; Imperial College of
Science and Technology, Department of Humanities (Dr
Marian Malet and Charmian Brinson); Imperial War
Museum (George Clout); R. L. Jenkins; R. V. Jones,
crew member of the 210 Squadron Sunderland; Herr

Wilhelm Kruse, wireless operator on *U48*; Lambeth Archives Department (Minet Library); Wg-Cdr F. F. Lambert, DSO, DFC, CD, RCAF (Retd); Joyce Ligertwood; London Library; Captain Karl-Friedrich Merten; National Maritime Museum; Naval Historical Branch, Ministry of Defence (R. M. Coppock and Lt-Cdr A. Hague); Eileen M. Paterson and Elizabeth Paterson; A. G. and S. A. Peard; Ronald Proyer; Royal Copenhagen Porcelain and George Jensen Silver Ltd; J. V. Sampson; *Sea Breezes*, the magazine of ships and the sea (Vol. 4, No. 24); Blake Simms, son of the late Commander Hugh Crofton Simms, DSO, RN (fatally wounded in action, December 1942), whose filial researches into the war record of HMS *Hurricane* revealed much fresh information on her crew and on the rescue and present whereabouts of *Benares* survivors; Edward R. Smith; E. J. Snoad; Southwark Administration; Guy Stafford; *This England* magazine; Transport, Department of, General Register and Record of Shipping and Seamen (Ms A. Williams); Jack Weir; Patricia B. Welch; John White.

British Library (newspapers)

National newspapers, and many provincial, local, and specialist newspapers, including: *Church Times*; *Kent Messenger*; *Liverpool Daily Post and Echo*; *Middlesex Chronicle*; *Richmond and Twickenham Times*; *Southern Echo* (Bournemouth and Southampton); *South London Press*; *South Wales Echo* (Mike Graham); *Sunderland Echo*; *The Universe*; *Wembley Observer*; *West Middlesex Gazette*.

Books

As It Happened, Clement Attlee (Heinemann, 1954)
Atlantic Ordeal, Elspeth Huxley (Chatto and Windus, 1941)

The Evacuees, ed. B. S. Johnson (Gollancz, 1968)

Exodus of Children, Derek E. Johnson (Pennyfarthing Publications, 1985)

From the Wings, Thelma Cazalet Keir (Bodley Head, 1967)

History of the Second World War, Problems of Social Policy, Richard M. Titmuss (Longmans/HMSO, 1950)

History of the Second World War, Vol. 1, No 14: The Naval War to the End of 1940, by Lt-Cdr Peter K. Kemp (Purnell, 1966)

Let Candles be Brought In, Geoffrey Shakespeare (Macdonald, 1949)

The Most Dangerous Gamble, John Sherlock and David Westheimer (Granada, 1982)

1940 – The World in Flames, Richard Collier (Hamish Hamilton, 1979)

The Nuremberg Trial, John and Ann Tusa (Macmillan, 1983)

The Scourge of the Swastika, Lord Russell of Liverpool (Cassell, 1954)

The War at Sea, S. W. Roskill, Vol. 1 (HMSO, 1954)

Who Will Take Our Children? The Story of the Evacuation in Britain 1939–1945, Carlton Jackson (Methuen, 1985)

Conference Proceedings

Lascars: The Forgotten Seamen, Conrad Dixon, from *The Working Men Who Got Wet* (Proceedings of the 4th conference of the Atlantic Canada Shipping Project, Memorial University of Newfoundland, 1980)

The Muscles of Empire: Indian Seamen and the Raj, 1919–1939, F. J. A. Broeze, from *Seamen in Society* (Proceedings of a conference of the International Commission for Maritime History, Bucharest, 1980)

Index